THE WOUNDED PILG

TO TRAVEL HOPEFULLY

TO TRAVEL HOPEFULLY

WRESTLING WITH VOCATION

❧

Anthony Faulkner

*To travel hopefully is a better thing
than to arrive, and the true success is
to labour.*

ROBERT LOUIS STEVENSON
Virginibus Puerisque vi 'El Dorado'

DARTON · LONGMAN + TODD

FOR PAM, AND FOR MY CHILDREN,
ROSE ELEANOR, THOMAS ANTHONY
AND JOSEPH STUART

First published in 1994 by
Darton Longman and Todd Ltd
1 Spencer Court
140–142 Wandsworth High Street
London SW18 4JJ

ISBN 0–232–52043–7

A catalogue record for this book is available
from the British Library

Cover design by Sarah John.

Phototypeset in $10\frac{1}{2}/12\frac{1}{2}$pt Bembo by Intype, London
Printed and bound in Great Britain
at the University Press, Cambridge

CONTENTS

FOREWORD

The 'Wounded Pilgrim' series is inspired by the belief that spiritual growth demands an openness to experience and a willingness to accept the challenge of self-knowledge despite the suffering, confusion and agony of spirit which this can involve.

Each author in the series has agreed to take the risk of exposing his or her vulnerability and inner struggle so that others may find comfort and support as they, too, seek the courage to continue on their own spiritual pilgrimage. The books are offered as nourishment for the many seekers in our society who yearn for understanding and encouragement but have all too often experienced the bewilderment or even the hostility of their co-religionists in the institutional Churches. Each writer in his or her own way attempts to respond to the call for a decade of evangelism or evangelization but does so out of the pain and woundedness which almost inevitably accompany the determination to be true to experience. There is no spirit of crusading or triumphalism to be found in these pages but rather the paradoxically fragile resilience of those who have not allowed their fear to prevent them entering the eye of the storm.

Anthony Faulkner knows what it means to hang on to hope in the face of apparent failure and intolerable emotional pain. His pilgrimage has been beset with disappointment and his endurance has sometimes been tested to breaking point. And yet the sense of being on a journey has never deserted him, even when the destination has seemed increasingly uncertain and the familiar landmarks have disappeared or revealed themselves to be little more than changing shapes in the mist. His calling to the Roman Catholic priesthood ended in resignation when he found he could no longer remain in office with integrity; his marriage finished when he accepted that the person he loved could no longer return that love and that what had begun in joyful freedom was now a kind of captivity. Many people would have succumbed to despair or reconciled themselves to a life without light. Anthony Faulkner, however, never completely lost the sense of his identity as the beloved of God. His experiences have strengthened his faith in the divine compassion and he has gradually learned that his deepest longing is to become the unique human being he has it in him to be. He is now a much loved and respected social worker, but for him, as for us all, the role is no longer of central importance. Our ultimate vocation is to accept that we are the beloved and to travel on in that knowledge however hidden our destination and however hazardous the journey. Woundedness then becomes not the mark of defeat but the channel of hope.

BRIAN THORNE

PREFACE

This book arose from a talk I gave to the Norfolk Theological Society entitled 'From Priest to Social Worker'. To my surprise, those present seemed to like it. The talk itself had its origin in a chance remark by a perceptive friend who said one day: 'It must be a bit tough, you've had two vocations and both of them have fallen through.'

I write to explain how it was that I came to be in this state of suspended animation, but much more, I hope, to encourage any kind reader who has also trodden upon stairs they thought were there and come a cropper.

If you manage to read to the end, I also hope you will perceive that I have no fundamental quarrel with the Catholic Church, but, so to speak, exercise the right of any family member to criticize his much loved family.

I wish to express my thanks to the editor, Brian Thorne, for inviting me to write this book in the first place and for being most helpful as the need arose. I am also very grateful to my father, my brothers, Richard and Bryan, and my friends, Peter and Joanne Harris, Nicholas and Janet Lash and Hubert and Clare Richards, especially the last, for their encouragement and practical help.

ANTHONY FAULKNER

1

VOCATION AND PRIESTHOOD

I imagine many ex-priests find themselves nervous at the prospect of writing or talking about themselves to a wider public. When people ask me what I did before becoming a social worker, and I tell them, there is a slightly embarrassed silence, then 'Oh! How interesting!' Sometimes my nerve fails me, as it did at a rather grand dinner party when a fellow guest tried to do some ice-breaking over the champagne:

'Good hunting your way?'
'I don't hunt.' (Pause)
'Haven't met your wife have I?'
'No, I'm afraid I'm divorced.' (Longer pause)
'You're a consultant, I believe?'
'Actually, I'm a social worker.'
'Oh!'

I hadn't the heart to tell this pleasant Catholic gentleman from the shires that for eighteen years I was a priest. Maybe he sensed it already, like the character in *Lipstick on the Host* (Aidan Matthews, Secker, 1992) who says in a Dublin bar about an alcoholic who had just come in: 'Like homosexuals, ex-priests and habitués of mental hospitals, I can always recognize them.'

The only justification I can find for writing about my life and failures is that I was asked to, and that it might throw a helping line to other people who also wonder who they are, how they got there and how they are going to cope. I am nervous, because I am well aware that Catholics, at any rate, invest a great deal in their priests, perhaps even more so thirty years ago than they do today. They afford them such status, such honour, such trust, that to resign from the ministry is something many Catholics, deep down, simply cannot comprehend. In this country a priest ideally is a member of every family yet belonging to none. He is with them at times of emotional sensitivity – baptism, reconciliation, eucharist, marriage, bereavement and death. He carries the secrets of the confessional as if they had never been told. He was trained for at least six years at their expense, literally, unless he was rich enough to pay for his own training. He usually depends on them financially if he works in a parish, as most do. He has no partner, no children to share his loyalty to them. How could I resign from this trust? Why did I become a priest in the first place? What did it feel like, being a priest?

My twin brother and I were born at Christmas time in 1933 into a family of three children, so that there were five of us under the age of six, and later a younger brother and another sister made seven of us under the age of fourteen. My father was then a somewhat remote figure, to be seen and not heard, anxious about providing for us all and generous with presents at Christmas. He did not discuss religion or our education. He had become a Catholic upon his marriage; in those days mixed marriages were frowned upon rather heavily. My mother was a devoted but unsentimental Catholic who had enjoyed most of her convent school days and who, like many girls brought up by the Holy Child nuns, remained incapable of telling a lie even for reasons of social convenience. The parish priest, seeing us all in the front row at mass, referred to her as Reverend Mother Faulkner.

We lived in a large old farmhouse in the country near Abingdon. Being Catholics, I think we never quite felt part of the village, though ladies and gentlemen living locally would call from time to time. We were a large family with a large garden and became rather self-sufficient. My mother somehow cultivated this enormous garden during the war to help feed us all, and an elder brother kept a cow to provide milk for us and for the grateful old ladies in the village. We were not hungry in those years, but we were very cold – underclothes, flannels and toothbrushes regularly froze during the night and to this day I dread having a bath because of memories of the cold. We would arrive frozen at school or church, and my twin and I often slept in the same bed to keep warm. We went to a good convent prep school three miles away, on the bus or bicycles, and later to a Catholic school ten miles away. I remember learning Latin grammar or French vocabulary with the book propped up on the handlebars, or reciting the rosary on these long rides. Life seemed uneventful; the war carried on, bombs fell near the house but never on it; we slept downstairs at times in case of a direct hit, though what good being downstairs would have done was not explained. Very little, in fact, was ever explained: it was a taken-for-granted world, no questions asked. Feelings were kept to one-self, and I still find it almost impossible to express anger or need or hurt, except when overwhelmed or taken completely by surprise, so I infer there was a general damping down of emotion, at least in my case.

At school, the sisters and later on the priests were nearly all unfailingly kind. However, as at home, questioning was not the order of the day. Whether it was a secular or religious lesson, the received knowledge or teaching was simply, though often quite brilliantly, handed down. I dwell on this lack of debate because I think it laid the ground for my ability later on to go to the seminary and remain passive throughout. That Catholics were in the right and everybody else in the wrong, even if inculpably so, was understood. This being split off from the culture and belief of most of my fellow human beings and countrymen did not strike me as strange at all – they hardly impinged upon my world. Looking back, I can see that in some ways I was strangely alone: I did rather well in exams but kept the academic life to myself as nobody at home seemed very interested. How could they be? Parents working hard to support us, my closest brothers more interested in the outdoors than the inner world of experience, my eldest sister (who was also gifted academically) seemingly inaccessible. The first real shock came when I was sixteen. The school had told me that I would be sure to win a scholarship to Oxford, and advised me to try for one before going to a seminary. However, the usual non-communicative network had been operating at home, and I was suddenly told by my mother that she had arranged for me to go to a junior seminary after doing school certificate. I wasn't surprised or appalled, but I remember wondering what had become of my talks with the headmaster about Oxford. In the previous year or two I had spent many weeks helping the parish priest around the church and grounds, and he too thought I should go to the seminary. He was a gentle, unsophisticated Irishman who also seemed unaware of the non-Catholic majority that makes up the human race, and with his blessing and £1 notes as frequent presents, off I went.

What is a vocation? Why did I agree to go to the seminary? Why did I stay there until ordination? After ordination, when I was miserable and lonely, why did I not complain? When after one year in the priesthood I realized I saw no value in being celibate, why did I stay on for a further seventeen years?

It is difficult to remember accurately how we felt when we were younger, and to avoid reading back into the past the various convictions that only come to be explicit much later in life. I think, too, that I am more of an extravert than an introvert. In my experience, introverted people have more accurate memories, and they keep diaries, photographs, postcards and other mementoes that provide autobiographical material. I have little such material. I tend to think and feel deeply when engaged in conversation, but not to remember much of it later on. I am forever being surprised when friends quote what I said years ago and have since forgotten. Nevertheless I feel sufficiently intrigued and encouraged to attempt some sort of answer to the questions.

When I was about eleven, we children (five boys and two girls) were at table with our parents. Somebody brought up the question of whether any of us would become a priest. My mother said: 'Well, I hope at least one of you will.' As I was the one who most often went to the church and indeed played at priests in my room with pretend altars, statues, holy pictures and so on, I remember thinking it would be me who would be ordained.

About a year before I went to the seminary at sixteen, my elder sister was teaching in a convent school run by the order of nuns who had trained her as a teacher. I remember her consternation, and my mother's, when she came home for the holidays and said she wanted to try her vocation and join the order herself. My mother gradually became resigned to losing her, but my father was pretty upset for a long time. He was talking to some new neighbours in the village, and, on being politely asked how many children he had, he replied, 'Five sons and a daughter – I did have another daughter.' 'Never mind, old chap, it happens in the best families,' was the misplaced response. My parents didn't see me as being lost to them in the same way. I suppose they knew that a secular priest would be free to keep in close touch with home in a way that nuns in those days certainly could not. My sister wasn't even allowed out to come to my ordination later on.

As far as I know, I wanted to be a priest because I felt close to God and wanted to help others to be the same. It was no sudden call, and I don't know when it was that I knew I had to follow it. I don't know whether, had I gone to Oxford, I would still have wanted to 'try my vocation' in a seminary afterwards. In those days, the early fifties, there were fewer choices open to young people: if you fell in love, you married; if you fell in love with God you probably thought you ought to become a priest or nun. Marriage was not seen as a vocation in the same league at all.

Holiness was not generally seen as a calling for everyone: you really had to be single-minded about it and that meant giving your life to God as a religious or a priest or both. This was the higher state of life to be in. If I and my contemporaries thought we might have a vocation we were unlikely to be told that we could serve God just as perfectly in the world. The implication was that holiness meant being out of this world, not in it. The attempt was made by the priests at college to reconcile being a priest with being in the world (unlike monks) with the explanation that we were to be 'in the world but not of it'. The expression was still used in common speech that so and so had 'gone into the Church', meaning that they had become clerics. Again the implication was that the other people were not 'in the Church' to the fullest extent. I shall come back to the subject at some length in chapter 8.

So I went off to the junior seminary, never having spent a night away from home before. As with so many people who go into professional training, or even on a course, my past was not acknowledged; it counted for nothing. I was as anonymous as a prisoner. The aim of the place was apparently to educate children from any age between eleven and eighteen in a Catholic classical way, to discern whether they had a vocation and to equip them for the senior seminary at eighteen. The building was late Victorian neo-Gothic, originally a convent school, beautifully polished and without any decoration whatever except for coloured plaster statues around every corner (we had to raise our biretta as we passed each one) and boring Arundel prints. Beeswax, pointed windows and starched cotton sheets were my first impression, as well as a warm ecclesiastical welcome from the rector who was an ancient, somewhat emasculated Victorian himself. He encouraged us daily to become 'holy, zealous and apostolic pweece' (*sic*). He read to us every evening, shrouded in his cloak, from a really ghastly book of Lives of the Saints. One evening I nearly exploded when he solemnly read that St Rita (I think it was) 'took to her bed and never rose again, except in ecstasy'. Laughter was never encouraged except at the Christmas concert. Another time he accidentally read a passage he had meant to leave out, and we heard how St Agatha had her breasts cut off. The poor man went as red as his cassock buttons and apologized. I touch on this because it reminds me that here we were, about sixty boys, boarding together for forty-six weeks of the year, and the subject of sex was never mentioned. Except, of course, in one's weekly confession when there would be some euphemistic way of saying one was troubled with impure thoughts or had 'abused' oneself. Here I am using the word 'one', automatically falling back into the avoidance vocabulary so common at the time. The atmosphere was curiously blended: warm rooms, good food, devotional chapel, tender and sentimental prayers, yet staffed by priests who remained totally separate from ourselves, never asked below the surface, never invited us to sit down in their study, never touched us in any way. Judging from what many older nuns have told me since, it was like a 1920s convent. Father Rector gave us an end of year talk before the summer holidays, instructing us to make our own beds, to save the maids work and to remind us that 'there is no holiday from God'. I escaped into academia, that is to say, alone and with the help of books I worked out how to read Latin easily, how to begin to understand Shakespeare, how to pray. Several times a week I would go down to the chapel during recreation and spend an hour in mental silence, sometimes crying from loneliness but at other times overwhelmed by the presence and love of God.

The testing of our vocation seems to have been a simple matter of observing whether a student 'kept the Rule'. The Rule ruled. Nobody asked where it had come from or what purpose it served. It was like the Ten Commandments, another shorthand way of preventing people from developing their own moral conscience. If a student kept the Rule, that is, he kept totally silent from 8 p.m. to 8 a.m. every day, was never late for meditation at 6.30 a.m., always walked about the grounds with at least two other students, never spoke to the nuns, did not keep chocolates overnight, questioned nothing, kept his cassock clean, and a hundred other such trivia, he was a conformist, he had a vocation! He was an obedient person, sound, trustworthy. He would become part of the Catholic establishment, so to speak. Qualities such as courage, initiative, adventurousness, humour, skill in communicating and listening – the gifts essential for pastoral work – were not held in esteem and certainly were not tested. Some mediocre students who kept the Rule for six or eight years or more were ordained although it was pretty obvious to fellow students that they were not suited to pastoral work at all.

I found all this conformism irksome in the extreme, being then, as fellows told me, a colourful character. They were practically all from suburbia and used to living among huge congregations with a well organized Catholic identity, lots of clubs, religion on tap like the Green Line buses. I came from rural and far away Berkshire where Catholics were scarce and individualized, where there were no groups or guilds or confraternities. I didn't like organized religion and the loss of freedom. I was very homesick. I missed the company of girls. I had only had one girlfriend, when I was about thirteen, which ended after our first kiss – I came over quite dizzy and unfortunately wiped my mouth and she saw that I did. But I dreamt of her and other girls, and envied my brothers who were in various stages of courtship and would bring their lovely girlfriends home. The only time my kind parish priest ticked me off was when he wrote after the summer holidays and told me to say the rosary every day (I didn't and don't like it) and not take my brother's girlfriend to the cinema in his absence. But I did love the idea of one day being a priest, and loved the liturgy, the life dedicated to God and the Church, the whole cultic mystery. So I stayed at the junior seminary for my two years, and passed Inter Arts even though we had to write the papers with a relief nib (a removable steel nib) – such was the Rule – and was apparently a model student.

I stayed, too, because no alternative interested me. My brothers went off and did their military service; later they somehow found themselves work in the retail side of motor cars (my father worked on the sales side at Morris Motors in Cowley) while my elder sister, now a professed nun, would soon become headmistress of a convent school. The world of business and education did not appeal to me. The spiritual world, the religious world, the Catholic world I found absorbing. At eighteen, our year of ten students moved up to the senior seminary. Here we had more free time to develop our interests to some extent, and the greatest pleasures I can remember were the afternoons or whole days when we could go off in threesomes and walk through the Surrey countryside, stopping at a pub for lunch or tea and covering anything up to twenty miles in a day. I made friendships with four or five others which have lasted until the present. I also loved the hours I would spend mowing the cricket pitch and tennis courts, which gave me endless time to think and to pray. Once a year we went into retreat – no study, total silence, just three conferences a day and the usual liturgical routine. I found I could just be with God for hours on end, perfectly content. But there were other days when I felt so bored and frustrated I nearly walked out; a diet of uninspired lectures on medieval philosophy, canon law, moral theology (which in those days had precious little to do with morality and even less to do with God) and dogmatic theology (dry scholasticism and Counter-Reformation apologetics mostly) was not my idea of a relevant training for the priesthood, even in the 1950s. The only course I really enjoyed was Church history, palatable partly because the books were in English, where all the others were in Latin. The lectures were somewhat biased in favour of what eventually came to be accepted as Roman Catholic orthodoxy or anyway conformity. I never actually read any Tertullian, or Nestorius, or Calvin or Luther in the original, only how they were regarded by Catholic authors. But the sheer scope of the subject, tracing the development of the Church from the earliest times to the present, did give me a framework within which to trace the course of European culture, and, like many Catholics, I feel I am at home in Italy or Hungary, Ireland or France, and have never had much admiration for little Englanders.

We did not just study the history of the Church, we felt very much part of it. We sang the Gregorian chant from the music and texts which were familiar to the monks from the sixth century and earlier. The Latin liturgy was largely unchanged from the early days of Christianity in the Roman and, later, Gallican Empire. We celebrated every day the feasts of saints dating from the time of the apostles. The Latin Vulgate Bible translated by St Jerome in the fourth century was as familiar to me as the Douai version in English. We experienced being Catholic in many senses of the word: continuous with the early Church, in living communion with the saints of the past and with the universal Church in the present, believing '*quod semper, quod ubique, quod ab omnibus creditur*' – 'what is believed always, everywhere and by all'. The papacy was both the symbol and, to a great extent, the guardian of this universality and unity.

So I stayed the course, sustained by friendship, a common purpose, idealism and the hope of ordination and freedom at the end. As senior student in the final year I was responsible for the good order of the students, representing their concerns to the rector and his to them as a sort of minor diplomat. This boosted my already quite sufficient self-esteem, and I looked forward, with the self-confidence arising from what amounted to a fundamentalist stock of certainties, to working as a priest in a parish. The ordination itself was beautiful and moving, though I felt strange being the sole ordinand in my home church and surrounded by family, friends and parishioners instead of ten other ordinands and ninety students in the choir, which was how it was done at college. Archbishop King was simplicity itself and as he was visibly showing his great age he sped through the ceremony so rapidly that I almost wondered whether the sacrament had really been conferred. Hundreds of priests from the diocese attended, but after the mass they all went off to dine with the bishop while I cycled the usual three miles home. Such was the clericalism of those days, there was no question of my family being invited to the clergy dinner. There was a profound sense in which I never really felt part of the clerical body from then on. Being a priest was fine, but being a cleric felt uncomfortable. I must say, however, that despite such incipient anti-clericalism I conformed to its mores for years and even wore the clerical collar on holidays at home, though not while camping abroad.

I felt wonderfully blessed when I said mass every day, even when I celebrated alone, in private. Such was the practice then, though it is highly unusual nowadays. I enjoyed preaching and administering the sacraments and was so keen to work that I supplied for a priest on holiday in the New Forest instead of taking the two months' leave I was offered.

The descent into the reality of my first curacy was about as great a contrast to the elation of the recent months as I could imagine. I don't know how to convey the sense of dismay, loneliness and misery arising from the lack of food, stark lodgings, virtual ostracism by the parish priest and neglect from other neighbouring priests. I was told that my boss had done wonderful work in the past, but in the present he appeared to me as cold and forbidding as the parish house and the church next door. A parishioner summed it up:

> When I came here and paid my respects to the parish priest, I went into his mean, dirty and decrepit house and told myself this man must be a saint. When I went into the church and found it equally dismal and neglected I told myself he was a mean old bastard.

His closeness with the cash was exemplified when, after two exceptionally cold, wet and snowy winters in which I covered six hundred miles a week on my moped, I used all my savings (£30) and bought a 1937 Morris Eight. It was dark blue and black and I was proud of it. I asked for extra petrol money (£2 a month was the previous allowance) upon which he lost his temper and said he would send me to a city parish if I ever asked that again. It wasn't easy to pay out of my own pocket as my salary was £5 a month and even in the late fifties that wasn't much. It had to buy clothing, books, tobacco (the one luxury), holidays and train fares on my day off when it would cost £2.15s (Cathedrals Express from Reading to Evesham return) to get home. The occasional offerings for baptisms and weddings helped, and better off colleagues sent offerings from time to time. I thought it rich when a neighbouring priest who lived in a very comfortable house, and to whom I put the problem, was unhelpful: 'You'll get a reputation as a money grabber if you're not careful.' I imagine this sort of put-down was common practice in professions in those days, but was disconcerted to find such a typical lack of friendly support from most colleagues. However, I saw little of them as I was in a remote village and none of them cared to visit me in my bed-sit.

What did make life rewarding was the friendship and love of parishioners. There were not very many of them, perhaps some three hundred in twenty scattered villages. I sought out the children and taught them in the schools and in Sunday groups. I couldn't find any interesting or suitable books for them (there is a plethora nowadays), and they ranged from Holy Communion age at seven to the oldest in the secondary schools. I discovered that the only way to hold their attention was to make up stories that incorporated elements of Scripture, doctrine, Church history and moral teaching. I visited families in the army camp ('Next time my wife has a baby I'll send it to the bloody Vatican'), on farms ('Two eggs or three, father?'), on council estates ('More tea?'), in cottages ('Have some apples to take back'), and in big houses ('How about a glass of brandy?'), and was given nothing but kindness and gratitude. I felt at ease with them all, and was especially impressed by the faith and patience and love in so many families where there were few material comforts.

It certainly helped me to accept my own sparse way of living. It was hard, though, to leave the warmth of a hearth and family late in the evening and return to my room, oil-stove and soup in a thermos.

Another hard experience was hearing confessions. Many Catholics went regularly through the year and all were expected to go at Christmas and Easter. Two or three priests would be on duty in the main church for six hours at a time, with a short break in between. This meant sitting in a cold, airless, dark confessional, unseen and almost disembodied, listening to a non-stop stream of people's problems, sins, guilt feelings, scruples, efforts at change, good resolutions. I never refused absolution because I assumed that each person was in good faith or they wouldn't have come at all. If they couldn't reach a point where they could realistically alter their behaviour, even though it might be quite seriously against official teaching, I still saw no reason to do anything but encourage and pronounce the words of absolution. They are, after all, ineffective if the person is in the wrong dispositions. I would emerge from these long sessions feeling humble before the sincerity and truthfulness of so many people, and exhilarated by knowing that at least a few hundreds of people felt renewed, relieved, reassured. The rather dangerous corollary was that I was doing hours of sketchy and hurried counselling, sometimes at a turning point in a person's life, without any training in counselling and, of course, without any supervision. The seal was and is absolute. It was, however, too easy to give well meant but inappropriate advice, to make an unhelpful suggestion, to ask a delicate question that proved the last straw for a tense or unhappy penitent. It was only some years later that I began to look more deeply into a religious system that tended to make people feel guilty in the first place and then benignly help them to be forgiven.

I felt needed and and depended upon to such an extent that I had to go on. I suppressed the anger I felt towards the old ladies in whose house I was suffered to lodge: they listened in when I used the telephone – I could hear the extension click – were patronizing to parishioners, and rude to hapless callers at the house. I had to use the house chapel, although there was a new one in the grounds, because it suited them better. Parishioners crowded into the stuffy, overheated room. One of the ladies was incontinent which didn't improve the atmosphere. At lunch, their table manners were disgusting. They drank wine and gave me water. I did all I could to avoid them and be civil when I could not. I suppressed, indeed, my anger towards so much of institutional Catholicism: the parish priest for sending me to this awful house in the first place, and giving me no support when I did see him; my fellow curate seven miles away who was a king-sized neurotic and drove me to distraction with his scrupulosity and his dependence on me, fifteen years his junior. I was angry about the Church teaching on contraception and divorce which made life impossible for many conscientious and lovely people and extremely painful for sympathetic priests who could not officially sanction their practice. I was angry at the wasted years at college: the idiocies of four years of dogmatic theology in which hours of lectures were spent on the processions in the Trinity, whether angels know our secret thoughts and whether there ever was a time when auricular confession was not practised in the early Church: the categorizing of sin in moral theology, and the division of the human body into *partes honestae and minus honestae*, that is, non-erogenous and erogenous. The genital areas were I think downright *dishonestae* – shameful. Canon Law had been another barren subject. For four years we went into the minutiac of the process of canonizing saints, the limits of spiritual jurisdiction, civil and ecclesiastical power and the rest. The 'spiritual life' was similarly coded and graded, tracing the journey of the soul through the 'purgative' way, the illuminative and finally (for the few) the 'unitive' way – not distinctions that were too handy for daily use in an English parish.

Great stress had also been laid on the dangers of particular friendships. I was once threatened with being sent away from the seminary because I spent too long laughing and talking with a student in his doorway. We were on no account allowed into each other's rooms: that *would* have meant instant expulsion. We could only go for walks in groups of at least three. The implication of course was that we were not to be trusted, that homosexuality was an ever present danger. Whatever else about those days, I knew very few students whom I even suspected to be inclined that way.

There were only two occasions when I can remember laughing during a lecture. One was when the lecturer (a kind old Irish priest intent on whitewashing the Borgia popes, pointing out that Alexander VI, notorious for his immorality and nepotism, had many redeeming features – didn't he, for instance, institute the practice of saying the Angelus three times a day?) asked a student to wake up the man next to him. The student looked about him and asked 'Which one?' The other occasion was seeing the consternation on another lecturer's face as he expounded *De Sexto* (the sixth commandment, for Catholics, is the adultery one). This man was an ascetic, well intentioned but devoid of the juices that render male humanity human. He carefully drew the female reproductive organs on the blackboard and, just as the second ovary was being put into place, a young student called Norman fainted with a loud crash. He was quietly removed from the room and from the college. Later on as a priest I could see some sense in that. I was more than once asked to go to the morgue to anoint a naked man or woman killed in a crash, and some of the confidences of anxious men and women in the confessional would have been pretty surprising if I hadn't known a lot about sexual perversion and variety. Sadly enough, most of what we were served up was of absolutely no use in preaching or instructing children or adults later on.

I was angry too because I hated being celibate. I used to dream of a girl in the parish and long to see more of her. She suffered too, but joined in the general conspiracy of silence and never said a word at the time. Perhaps, even more than celibacy, I hated living alone, isolated, unsupported. I suppose I was still emotionally a boy, projected from family life to college life but with no development to prepare me for independent living, facing myself and the world with which I really wasn't connected; in the world but not of it; part of a sacred caste yet – alone. Occasionally I would go to a monastery, Douai near Reading, or Farnborough, and talk to a monk. It struck me how balanced and friendly and normal the Benedictines were, and how much they valued and depended upon a community life. It never occurred to me that perhaps I should have been a monk. I felt strongly that for me pastoral work was of the nature of the priestly ministry, and teaching boys in a public school or tending the plant in a contemplative monastery didn't seem to me to be much to do with the priesthood at all. I still think the same. By all means have monks, especially Benedictines, but why ordain them unless they have a community to minister to?

I was angry that I had no garden to walk in, and no time for exercise – not that I have ever enjoyed physical exertion very much. There was no *leisure* and no one to be leisurely with, so I drove myself more and more into work because time alone would otherwise have been unbearable. I was angry with my parents who saw my distress and did nothing about it. They could have said (I thought), 'Go and talk to the bishop about this hell hole you're in, and if you don't we will.' I didn't really blame them in fact, because Catholics in those days would have felt unable, as 'mere lay people', to interfere with ecclesiastical matters. They did not comment on how unhappy I looked and how much weight I had lost. I probably had a *noli me tangere* (don't touch) air about me anyway to inhibit them and anybody else who might have sought to help. I'm sure I did.

All this anger I suppressed and denied. I wanted to be a good priest and if it meant some suffering then that was all part of sharing in the suffering of Christ for the good of others. Anger denied, I have since learned, will produce anxiety if the anger is powerful enough, anxiety that may amount to panic. The shouting and screaming that woke me one night was a severe panic attack, three years after being in that awful house. I thought I was dying. My limbs were cold and numb and I couldn't stop screaming. I sat up all night in terror and the old ladies next morning sent for a doctor whom I knew and liked and whose wife was a parishioner. He could find nothing physically wrong but was kind enough to go and see the parish priest and tell him I needed a long rest. What I got was a fortnight, while word went round on the clerical circuit that I was a nervous wreck, over-sensitive, overreacting. I spent the time at home and my mother gave me port to cheer me up and give me some strength because I complained of feeling weak. At the time I drank only on social occasions, so the port allowed me days of sleep which were the only relief from the constant fear and terror of waking hours. I wished with all my being that I were dead. I tried to read Shakespeare's tragedies, of all things, but the characters seemed unreal – everything was unreal, and I felt that nobody could or did have the slightest idea of how terrible I felt. I cannot imagine how I managed to return to the horrible place, but I did, and before many months I sat in my room one night and again thought I was dying. This time I had a huge swelling in the throat and couldn't swallow. I had not then heard of psychosomatic illness or hysterical paralysis (who had, in 1961?), but I went to my own doctor whose name was Dr Trust. I had not seen him professionally before, but his name and kind manner encouraged me to tell him in detail not only how my average days were spent but also something of how I felt. He said that if I carried on as I was I would break down seriously. After another rest and some barbiturates I was able to go back to work, but happily the old bishop had by this time heard what was happening and wrote me a line in his shaky handwriting: 'Dear Tony, I hope to give you a nice move soon, so try to carry on.' He enclosed a £5 note, the large white one I'd not handled before. It seemed to give me courage and I waited for the move.

I was now twenty-seven. A few days before moving to Reading I went over to see the new parish priest. He gave me a warm patriarchal welcome and what he called the good news – my salary (much more generous), the warmth of the parishioners, the routine work, and introduced me to the housekeeper, a lovely young country woman from Tipperary. Then I went upstairs to see the outgoing curate and hear the bad news. It wasn't bad at all, just more about the work and how happy he had been there. I couldn't quite believe I would be in a normal, pleasant household with a large room and next to a fine Pugin church. After a few months of this atmosphere I felt healed and restored. All through the bad times I had continued to pray longer than ever. I knew it was a source of strength, but it didn't make me feel any better. The feeling of well-being returned because 'J P', the new priest, gave me his trust, approval and affection. I am sure that God nearly always reaches us and makes us whole through human beings. It is his normal way and a central feature of the divine economy. So many Christians seem to look to Jesus for salvation but fail to find him where he is usually to be found, in their neighbour. I once knew a nursing home run by this kind of person. It was a loveless place. Matron's study had captions all over it saying 'Jesus Loves You'. If only she had herself she could have put the captions away.

J P had a sense of humour. He used to go out for a walk of an evening and have a pint in the local hotel. One evening I left him a note: 'Canon, am out, with the Flanagan problem'. I returned late to find the answer: 'Father, am in, with no problem'. The parishioners were nearly all Irish and most of them were not, as they would say, scholars. J P told me he had invited his friend Ronald Knox to conduct a parish mission two years before. I said, 'I can't imagine they enjoyed that.' He replied, 'No, but I did.' Shortly before he died, of heart failure, he gave me a long sideways look and announced: 'My friends are pressing me to retire, and I've told them that I've thought it all over and am determined to go on until my curate drops.' When he suddenly died I was devastated. My previous father figure, the parish priest of my student days, had also died and I felt alone again. J P's successor was a sad contrast, theologically strait-jacketed and dogmatic, a paranoid alcoholic and ill at ease with parishoners. He used to lose his temper in the pulpit and it drove many of them away from the church. In particular I hated the way he undermined the work of the gentle headmaster of our junior school. He and his staff had worked out with me an entirely new approach to preparing children for their first confession and communion. The parish priest ignored this entirely and questioned them on the catechism instead, with the result that their first communion had to be prepared for all over again in the narrow, boring, unintelligible old way. He was equally insensitive towards parents who did not support the Catholic schools. I was unwise enough to say how sorry I was that an Italian mother had lost her husband in an accident. Next day he told me he had been to see her and had told her off for not sending their boy to the Catholic school. I felt physically sick when eventually I had a showdown over similar matters and the bishop, instead of moving him to where he might do less harm, moved me instead to a new parish where I would be happier. I hadn't realized that bishops can be intimidated by autocratic parish priests just as much as the curates who have to share a house with them can be. But at least I had expressed my anger to the priest and to the bishop, which was a breakthrough for me. The pernicious effect of nearly four years in that tense, cold household (the Irish housekeeper had long since left and married) was lasting. Out of eight years in the priesthood, less than two of them had been a good experience as far as immediate superiors were concerned, and I felt I had little sympathy from colleagues to whom I tried to describe how frustrated I felt. In psychological terms, my eight years in the seminaries with pleasant companions but remote, very clericalized lecturers, and the subsequent experiences in parish life with no companions to offset two ghastly parish priests, meant that I never built up a basic trust in the clergy. It would be one of the decisive factors in my later resignation from the ministry.

Meanwhile, the next three years were happy as far as living in the presbytery was concerned. My good personal experience with Joe, the parish priest in Fareham, and with my fellow curate, somehow couldn't get me over this block, this lack of trust. Distrust was also fed by most of the clerical priest friends of Joe who came to the house and were suspicious of change, fearful their authority was being undermined, contemptuous of curates, especially English ones. Joe and his circle were Irish. However, there were times of pure bliss, when for instance Joe and I would go off for a picnic on the downs together with Pat the housekeeper who had prepared a hamper with cold chicken, salads and wine by the gallon. There were also nights when neither Joe nor I could sleep, awakened perhaps by traffic noise. We would meet in the Aga-warm kitchen and he would fetch up a new bottle of Scotch. It is amazing how much of the stuff you can drink without ill effects, provided you add hot water and lemon and the conversation is good. We sometimes spent the whole night talking and laughing in this way. Another moment of pure, though wicked joy was when Gedge – the colourful, ex-Anglican curate – came back a bit shaken from an accident. He had been visiting in the dark, riding his scooter over rough potholes in Warsash, and the next thing he knew was that he was flying through the air into an oncoming car. He told us that the driver took him home and said to his wife, 'I was driving along slowly and the next thing I saw in my headlights was a bloody parson coming through my windscreen.' Gedge wasn't hurt: he has a bullet of a head which sometimes got him into trouble. He would butt the bishop with it. He had a love–hate relationship with bishops and theologians. In his next parish he lived frugally and worked very hard. The bishop and his chaplain were staying overnight, so Gedge gave them his only two bedrooms and put up a tent on the lawn for himself. He rather spoilt it all, however, by hoovering the bishop's bedroom at 5.30 the next morning, as if to make a point. When I return to this part of Hampshire I still think I am in the Gedge, not the Strong country.

I have banged on here about clericalism, because it frightened me and still does. It came out in various unlovely forms that I thought exaggerated the status of the priest who is, after all, a minister to and at the service of the Church. One example was of the young artist who used to sit at J P's feet, listening to his words of wisdom, but also preparing his meals when Peggy was away. After J P died she proudly showed me a book he had given her with the inscription: 'To G–, for being my Martha and my Mary'. A priest is taught to think of himself as *alter Christus* – another Christ – in his sacramental role, but this was pushing it a bit. Another example was my repeated experience that whatever excesses a priest fell into, with women, or drink, or scandalous behaviour, the important thing was to protect 'his' priesthood. Let him be moved, let it be hushed up, but don't tell him to resign. That would be even more scandalous. I knew, indeed loved one priest who said he would do anything, even go to hell (!) rather than give up his priesthood. This trait was particularly strong among men from traditionally Catholic cultures and has become a huge scandal recently with the court actions being brought against priests in England, Canada and America in particular. Properly understood, the sense of the sacredness of the priestly state gave them an aura of authority and self-confidence, but when it was abused it led to moral blackmail, arrogance and, worse, unlovely manners described sufficiently in our contemporary press and television programmes.

I was not myself without faults in this direction. During these three years I certainly wobbled on the tightrope between my human, sexual and emotional needs so long ignored and my role as a trusted sacral figure. I began a relationship with a girl which, although pretty mild in normal heterosexual terms, was one that I wouldn't have wanted known about. I split it off from the rest of my official image and behaviour. What was worse was that she wasn't the only one. I was emotionally in my teens although now thirty-five years old.

It was in this confused state that I arrived at Park Place in 1969, to be the Director of a new pastoral centre.

2

PRIESTHOOD AND RESIGNATION

When the bishop, with his usual courtesy, asked whether I would consider taking on the directorship of Park Place, my initial reactions were mixed. I told him I knew I would enjoy a new and exciting venture, and that I felt confident that I could both attract good speakers and also give retreats and conferences myself. Unlike many of my contemporaries, who were burying their heads in the sand until the storms of Vatican II and the new theological and liturgical ideas fermenting on the main European continent died down, I had continued to keep abreast. But I also said that I hated having to be celibate, and that the warmth of parish life was some protection against the emotional isolation celibacy demanded. I remarked ungraciously that I did not want to live in a convent with a community of French nuns, even if it was now to be called a Pastoral Centre. Further, I didn't like their cooking, which wasn't French at all but indifferent English. It is interesting how small observations such as these often symbolize a deeper apprehension. In the end, seven years later, I resigned because I felt theologically out of sympathy with mainstream, conservative Catholicism, in England anyway, and because celibacy had become a meaningless burden and I was lonely. It was also expecting too much of the community that either their cooking or their kindness could sustain me in what were to be intellectually and emotionally the most exacting years of my life.

At the time I dimly realized what later I came fully to believe: that spiritual strength usually comes to us through natural support systems and other human beings. If I had been able to choose three or four companions and live as part of a team of priests and pastoral

19

workers I might perhaps have survived. There would at least have been others to tell me to stop throwing my weight about, not to become overstretched, to take little sabbaticals. There would have been times to relax and laugh and pray together. This may sound too idealistic, but the opposite extreme, of being one priest-director in a position of considerable influence and responsibility living alone among and yet separate from the sisters and fellow priests outside the centre, proved too much for me in the end. When I did resign, there were inevitably those who had seen it coming, who implied that I had given up prayer and orthodox faith. I want to make the point that, on the contrary, I spent more time than ever all through those years in prayer and reflection, and that the theological explorations I engaged in were an attempt to present a faith with relevance to the changed world of the 1970s rather than an exercise in undermining or attenuating it. It is a truism that if you just repeat old formulae you don't preserve them at all if they cease to convey a meaning. 'In a higher world it is otherwise; but here below to live is to change, and to be perfect is to have changed often' (John Henry Newman). I also want to say that the same would hold for many of my priest friends who resigned at about the same time.

With these rather defensive comments out of the way, I would like to try and describe in some detail how I felt the process of change within myself, and how it forced me to take the radical step away from the priestly ministry and the clerical, ecclesiastical world. I hope this will not be tedious for the reader. I know that the autobiographies of former priests which focus almost exclusively on what they were accomplishing rather than on what they were experiencing, have left me unmoved. I didn't seem to know the authors any better at the finish than at the beginning. I also know from daily experience that when people talk about their own inner world they interest me, and my relationship with them changes for the better. The then Anglican bishop of Portsmouth became my friend the day he and I stood in front of a large gathering of his clergy which he was to address. Just before I rose to welcome and introduce the subject of his address he turned and whispered: 'Was it Wellington on surveying the troops who said "I don't know what effect these men will have upon the enemy, but, by God, they terrify me"?' Such revealing incidents endear us to the real person beneath the workaday front.

The outer world I have described briefly in chapter 1. As the Pastoral Centre began to host conference after conference and I gave talk after talk, I experienced a quite new understanding of the Church. I was living with it. Previously I had only known the parish model, families nurturing the faith (or not) in private but coming together (or not) on Sunday to be ministered to and sent away again. There were societies and groups and classes during the week which I might visit or talk to and then go away again. Similarly, there were various working parties and commissions that brought people together for *ad hoc* decision-making or planning. Now, however, I found myself throughout the year living among a group for three or more days and with them experiencing an astonishing growth in awareness, in faith, in understanding that might change the course of their and my life. Even more powerful was the celebration of the eucharist which was now to have a reality I had not known before, because it signified and deepened the sense of communion already reached by the group. This of course soon meant that the usual liturgical moulds were just not suitable for such intensity of human joy and unity. We avoided extremes, but the differences between a parish mass and a shared group mass where everybody already felt close to each other was profound. There were complaints made to the bishop, of course, as somebody or other couldn't accept that passing the chalice around the room, or leaving out the creed, or not wearing vestments were not somehow invalidating the whole thing.

Another difficult area was intercommunion with other Christians. It is perhaps just about understandable that, as long as the mainstream churches are in fact separated, their members may not share the eucharist which symbolizes unity. But in a pastoral centre Catholics, Anglicans, Methodists would be talking and praying and learning together for days at a time and so building up what was, for the time being anyway, a real sense of community, *koinonia*. How could they not be allowed to celebrate this sacramentally? Like many priests in my position, I took the view that charity came first and the rules second.

I also gave a liberal interpretation to other rules. At the time we were only supposed to let people receive from the chalice on very special occasions. I reckoned every conference was a very special occasion. One Sunday there was a large group being addressed by a supposedly eminent liturgist. I had prepared three chalices on the altar so that the congregation, as was our practice, could help themselves if they wished. It always worked reverently and people appreciated it. It served as a small but clear signal that they were a priestly people. I was dismayed when the speaker came in and, in front of everybody including myself, swept the chalices off the altar with an angry 'This is not allowed'. None of this 'Take and drink, all of you' for him. On another occasion the practice caused me some embarrassment. It was a conference of somewhat conservative men who came for the day. As there were 120 of them I prepared three full chalices. Absolutely nobody drank from them. Mother Francis and I spent a long time afterwards talking about spiritual matters while we slowly drank the contents.

It took two years of hard work to get enough bookings to fill the Centre all the year round. In my first year I had advertised a conference for Catholic and Anglican nuns, a new idea in those days. Nobody booked! After hours of telephoning hundreds of convents we did manage to launch the weekend for twenty nuns and it was a moving experience. Most of them had never met a counterpart from the other tradition. They found, of course, that what they had in common completely overshadowed their differences. Gradually, with several outstandingly successful events behind us, word got round that Park Place was a good thing and people enjoyed going there. In my first year our annual turnover was less than £1000. In my last it was well over £40,000.

For better or worse, Park Place declericalized me. I often wore a cassock and collar (they are most comfortable garments) but just as often a roll-neck and flannels. People never quite knew what to expect. They often mistook me for the gardener when I was mowing the two-acre lawn. On one occasion my bishop was bringing a very conservative bishop to see the place. He told me afterwards that he had spent a good deal of the journey persuading the visiting bishop that even if Anthony was in casuals he was a good chap really. In fact I had put on my cassock and couldn't understand why the visitors looked confused.

Following *Humanae Vitae* (the encyclical on birth control) at first a trickle, later a stream of priests and religious resigned from their vocational state of life. Those who really could not give inner assent to the papal teaching were in a double bind. They could not in public say anything that threw the teaching into question, so they were outwardly supposed to be conforming to it. If in the confessional they were giving contrary advice or passive encouragement to the use of contraception, they felt uneasy. It was a sort of collusion between priest and penitent. People shopped around for a confessor known to be sympathetic. Few priests felt able to come out into the open with the truth of what they thought. After a while many people gave up bothering and made up their own minds, but the priest still felt the tensions of inwardly believing one thing while outwardly he was presumed to be conforming to the papal line. Priests like Charles Davis resigned because they could not accept Rome's assertion that the Church was not divided on the matter. Davis said it was a plain lie to pretend it wasn't. There were plenty of priests, too, who were unhappy to see the pressure brought to bear on theologians who held posts in Catholic universities (it is a blessing that we have none in England, but much the same pressure was and is put on teachers in Catholic schools) and who lost their posts because they challenged official teaching on the subject, as well as on the current discipline on divorce and remarriage, intercommunion and celibacy. These resignations affected me very much for I knew and liked many who were leaving. But, until 1975, I simply did not entertain the thought of leaving myself. 'I must go on!' I remember saying to a priest counsellor who was helping me in the severe difficulties I got into in a relationship with a younger woman. He went through reasons and motives and alternatives in what I thought was pitiless detail, but it didn't shake me even though I was causing great pain to the woman concerned.

I was changing in various ways. The work of the Centre, with thousands of people coming each year, was a heady experience. I was not inclined to the charismatic style at all, more to a freeing up of confined dogmatic positions, and of buried emotions. Not that I was one of the 'let it all hang out' school either, but there is no doubt that the ethos of the Centre and my part in it did encourage openness, warmth, expression of feeling, questioning of monumental dogmatic assumptions. Time and again people said how relieved they were to hear someone in an official position voice their unspoken convictions. I knew, however, that I was walking a tightrope. One weekend I was giving talks to nuns who were preparing to become eucharistic ministers, that is, to distribute Holy Communion at mass and take the sacrament to sick people at home. I was trying to show that Christ is present in all sorts of real ways besides being really present in the sacrament itself. I was actually presenting ordinary traditional theology. But the chaplain to the nuns was there, constantly challenging me and implying that I was watering down the unique doctrine of the real presence, ready, no doubt, to report back to the bishop. I didn't mind if he did, as the bishop always backed me, but I felt threatened all the same by what the chaplain represented.

Other priest friends went through a far worse grilling than I ever did. I watched Peter Harris forced out of the seminary where he had done his best to bring the place into the post-Vatican II world. I saw Hubert Richards being cornered for his alleged unorthodoxy and forced out of a college where he had been the leader and inspiration for years, a college which was a model in Europe and to which many priests and nuns and teachers were profoundly grateful, and still are to this day. Nobody in authority seemed to stand up for such intelligent and patently honest priests. They are only two examples of the many I knew about, and this was under the relatively mild pontificate of Pope Paul VI. I would never have survived myself under the regime of the present pope and Roman curia. On the other hand, equally enlightened priests like David Konstant, Jim Brand, John Coventry and many more were able to continue within the system and taught me a great deal. In the end, I suppose it comes down to how much a person can tolerate and live with. I do not wish to give the impression that I was always unhappy and without support. But, much as I came gradually to appreciate the company of some fellow diocesan priests, let alone religious priests and married people and students, I still felt an odd man out. It was as if all my friends were seen as a bit peculiar, a bit way out.

When a priest leaves the ministry it comes as a shock to many people, but is in fact the end of a process of distrust, disintegration and dissatisfaction rather than a sudden change of direction. In my case I think the main contributory factors were threefold. The first was the theological revolution going on in the Church's understanding of herself. This gave rise to all sorts of consequences, but the element I want to concentrate on at present is the overarching theme of Vatican II, that the Church consists of the people of God, a priestly, pilgrim people. To nurture, support and minister to this people, some of them are called to be ordained as priests and bishops, and the unity of the communion of local churches is symbolized by the office of the Bishop of Rome (the ancient title of the pope, happily brought into use again by the popes of the Council). This emphasis on service should be reflected in the liturgy. Hitherto the priest had been the hierarch, the intermediary between the people and God, standing with his back to the people and doing sacred things on their behalf but himself sacred and apart. Now he would be required to face the people, more like a father or mother presiding at table and seeing that everyone played their own part and would be sufficiently nourished by word and sacrament. At the same time, Vatican II gave a new importance to the manifold ways in which members of the Church should share in the ministry. Priesthood was no longer to be the supreme route to God, the loftier vocation. Marriage was to be given far more status as a holy state of life through which the Church would be built up and her teaching and life passed on. Many clergy resented the apparent down-grading of their office and position, and tensions ran high in the seventies. Shortly before I resigned, Adrian Hastings wrote in *The Tablet* (15 May 1976) summarizing 'The priesthood today' in two masterly articles. I would like to quote a passage that I felt exactly articulated some of the tension I felt myself under at the time:

> The basic issue is not an individual but a theological and a structural one: clerical training, workload and life style had come to take on a rather tight pattern, reflecting a highly clericalist theology of the ministry. Basically the clerical structures of the first half of the 20th century have been sharply punctured both by a renewed theology (largely accepted by the theory though less by the practice of Vatican 2) and by a wider social and educational revolution in the world. Younger and more thinking priests grow more and more conscious with the years that if they stick to a fairly conventional pattern of ministry they are in danger of being left high and dry, in terms of the theological and social revolution, while if they respond to the latter they become alienated from the institution as it now is. This sense of a deep dilemma of which older ecclesiastical superiors seem simply unaware can be as strong in the men who remain as in those who leave. For such problems there is no easy answer, although we would be vastly helped by a clearer distinction between the religious-monastic

and the diocesan-pastoral vocations, and by exorcising the unreasoning fear of allowing the same man to be both priest and husband.

The second contributory factor towards my eventual resignation was celibacy, a symbol for me not of dedication but of isolation. Despite the tensions described by Adrian Hastings, and despite the liberalizing of my understanding of Scripture which led to the kind of questioning so courageously tackled a decade before by John Robinson in *Honest to God* and the ensuing debate, I think I could still have continued in the priesthood if I had had the support and company of a wife. There was and is no question but that I love the Church and wish to be of use in it. What I was not coping with were the combined pressures of being sniped at as liberal and theologically unsound, of being endlessly available to groups and individuals all the year round in a very public manner (even my study was not private: guests would peer in through the barrel bay windows, and when I did eventually get to bed I was often wakened by rowdy conferencees or their children), and of feeling emotionally attracted by and attractive to many different girls or young women. If at the end of a long day a trusted and valued woman friend came to my room, I had not the moral courage to say 'I must finish my breviary (official prayers) and go to bed, goodnight'. Not that I blame any of these friends. It was my fault or my need that led me sometimes to take the initiative, with results that were occasionally disastrous and deeply unsettling for both parties. There were hysterics and cover-ups, dishonesty and dilemma. There was the most acute embarrassment when the two worlds I had mentally kept so separate clashed, the two worlds of ecclesiastical rectitude and my human need. I had become too intimate with a girl still at school, and just as she was about to leave school at eighteen her father found an incriminating letter and gave my bishop hell. The bishop sent for me. I thought, insouciantly enough, that he might want to sound me out about my future, to ask whether I would take on a different kind of work. Instead, he confronted me with my letter and the father's outrage. I felt like a schoolboy caught in the act by a trusting headmaster. But what really did the damage was his comment: 'You are a good priest, it would be a tragedy if you left.' I had never consciously looked at the possibility of leaving, nor supposed anybody else had.

Perhaps I should have told him exactly how I felt, and how impossible it was for me to carry on where I was. I did not do so. I could not let go and talk. So I expressed regret, exonerated myself as far as possible, told him nothing disastrous had taken place – the usual things, I suppose. They were true of course. Like my mother, I may not say the whole truth but I certainly cannot tell a lie. He gave me a whisky and told me to get away from the place completely and have a good holiday.

I went to old friends who are staunch Catholics and who live in a somewhat stately home in a very unstately way. To them I owe the greatest gratitude. I gave them hints of what was troubling me, but they asked no questions. They gave me the oldest room in the house and put what seemed like tree trunks on the fire by which I sat all day, huddled in a sheepskin. They left me alone. I would come down to the kitchen some time in the morning for fresh sardines or eggs or whatever was going. Then back up to the sanctum. Some lunch appeared, then more rest in the afternoon. At 6 p.m. the parents and any of the family would appear and we would celebrate the eucharist round a little table. After that we had some drinks and dinner.

Letters arrived from the distraught girl who didn't know what had really happened as her father hadn't told her that he had complained to the bishop. All she knew was that the latter had told me not to see her again. I wrote back as best I might, not knowing whether the letters would be intercepted. It was a bad, bad time. After two or three weeks of this complete rest I went back to Park Place, to being on show, the 'good priest' who had needed a break from work and was now better. The forbearance of the sisters, some of whom had an idea of what was going on, astonished me. The problem, however, remained. I was not facing the contradiction, apparently pretty shameful and shabby, of being one sort of person in public and another in private. And I felt that there was no one in authority to whom I could turn for sensible advice. The bishop, for all his patent good will, was not someone I felt I could talk openly with. It was not his fault, but neither was it mine. I was growing emotionally and getting in touch with buried feelings rather late for comfort; that was the difficulty. I did try to consult fellow priests, but, as usual, they told me of their own troubles before I found the opportunity to tell them of mine. By that time I was the counsellor and didn't feel able to switch roles and become counsellable myself. I suppose something in me presents as able to manage, appears above or beyond that sort of help. It has been a feature throughout my life, though I was soon to learn how to accept help. Until then I either could not ask for it, or I needed to be the giver of help more than I thought I needed to be helped. In the Acts of the Apostles the Lord Jesus himself is quoted as saying that 'it is a more blessed thing to give than to receive', but I no longer believe that it applies on every occasion.

Despite this crisis, I still hadn't realized that I was at a crossroads and would have to make a decision. I went back to being the competent director of a flourishing pastoral centre. There followed a time when I was dog tired from the organizing of conferences and the giving of talks. Part of me felt proud and pleased to be in charge of such a successful venture, touching the lives of so many people who were obviously gaining much from their days with us. Part of me felt absolutely alone. This was epitomized by my annual return from a holiday with friends, usually to France or Italy. From the warmth of living in a group of three or four for three weeks I would come back to a place that had closed for a while and reverted to being an old-fashioned convent. My room was polished and tidy and dead. The retriever was overjoyed to see me. Reverend Mother was welcoming. The correspondence was overwhelming, letter upon letter of bookings, personal troubles, unwanted professions of affection, and I was – alone. There was also my mother's inability to understand that I had left home for many years, that my interests and ties lay elsewhere, that friends came first because they were the ones I could talk to. This caused bitterness and opprobrium and was hard to accept. Looking back, I think she was frightened intuitively on my behalf, but because the Pastoral Centre was so successful it must have been daunting for even close relations to criticize or ask me whether I was perhaps skidding in the fast lane.

It was not very long before I fell seriously in love. My elder sister was at the time the principal of a training college in London and her students used to come to Park Place for conferences. In the group that came this particular year were several young women whose outlook and understanding of the Church were very much the same as mine, and among these new friends was Debbie, with whom I established a particular rapport. I perceived her as uncertain of herself and looking for some understanding and support.

She saw me in turmoil and generously sought to stabilize me after the emotional time I had, to some extent, survived. These, anyway, were the conscious motives. After our second long talk I told her that I loved her.

This, so far as I can honestly remember, is how matters rested when I was about forty. Gentle reader, as Trollope might have written, you may well ask, 'Oh God, isn't he ever going to grow up?' It would take me a little time yet, I fear.

At about the same time a third factor began to operate. I came to know a number of gifted psychiatrists and allied professionals who had established a psychotherapy society which they invited me to join. In those days, the past so recent and yet so far away, counselling and psychotherapy had only begun to make their presence felt in England. A whole new literature in this genre has since become familiar, but at the time it was new, certainly to me. I did courses, joined encounter groups, learned to say 'I' instead of 'you' or 'one'. In short, I was helped to become aware of and take my affective life seriously. Feelings may be an unreliable guide when we come to make decisions. They vary, and may depend on ephemeral experiences and influences. That was no good reason why they should for so long have been relegated to the dustbin in our culture. I already knew the cost of keeping the upper lip stiff and soldiering on, because it led to serious physical illness on occasion. At times I had been dependent on tranquillizers when the symptoms became unbearable. Now I was to find that I could begin to tell the inner truth to and about myself in the safety of a small group. They did not laugh at me, were not surprised or appalled. There was no blame, only encouragement to talk and talk. I found this process liberating; it was like coming out of a dense and stifling fog; it was a recapturing of lost childhood, a difficult but rewarding way of learning to trust the feelings both of myself and of others. Feelings carry no responsibility: they are not good or bad, right or wrong. They just are. The relief was so great that I felt quite young again. During a four-day workshop I was listening to another member of the group saying how much he was missing his wife. I found myself saying, 'How do you think I feel? I've been lonely all my adult life.' At that point I saw very clearly that I would have to change the direction of my whole life. I would have to choose to live and not deny whole areas of myself. I told the group the next day that I had decided to leave the priesthood, having spent most of the previous night discussing it with the senior psychiatrists present. It was the last of the four days, and for all of us the experience had been both painful and joyful and incredibly creative. The small groups of eight, about sixty people in all, celebrated in the conference hall with dancing and music. For the first time in my life I danced, naturally and fluently, hour after hour.

Having made the decision, I gave myself a year to fulfil commitments already made and to negotiate some sort of future for myself. The unthinkable became not only possible but amazingly easy. I told Debbie of my decision to leave, and later asked if she would marry me. I went to various people to seek advice about a professional career. If I had had money I would have sought a serious psychotherapeutic training at the Tavistock Institute, but as I could not envisage going out into the world alone I decided to apply for social work training and marry at about the same time. Being accepted by Suffolk College and funded by the Home Office presented no difficulty. Debbie's parents were welcoming and supportive. The most touching and surprising thing was that, once it became known I was shortly to leave the Centre and resign from the ministry, a large number of individual friends wrote and sent cheques to see me through. One nun, president of a large college, said in a sentence: 'It is really true that you are leaving? I disapprove, but here is a cheque to help you on your way with thanks from a grateful staff.' The parish priest from Reading, where I had been a curate, sent a kind letter and cheque for £300 'from a grateful parish'. Officially, that is, from the diocese, there was no mention of help, no question of how I would manage after eighteen years of service to the Church. But from the Church that really mattered to me, individual, warm, non-judgemental people, I received not only understanding but enough money to buy a cottage outright before we married.

It was making the decision that was difficult. Once made, the advice of Goethe, whose *locus* I cannot trace, was realized fully:

> Until one is committed, there is hesitancy; the chance to draw back: always ineffectiveness, concerning all acts of initiative and creation.
>
> There is one elementary truth, the ignorance of which kills countless ideas and splendid plans: that the moment one definitely commits oneself, then providence moves too. All

sorts of things occur to help one that would never otherwise have occurred. A whole stream of events issues from the decision, raising in one's favour all manner of unforeseen incidents and meetings and material assistance which no man could have dreamed would have come his way.

Whatever you can do, or dream you can, Begin it: boldness has genius, power and magic in it.

Begin it now.

There were three people I dreaded telling, however: the bishop, my mother and my nun sister. The bishop had been moved to another diocese but he telephoned, distressed, asking me to come and see him and talk it over. I rather abruptly declined as I didn't want to explain myself in depth and did not feel I could make myself understood anyway. My sister was calm and kind as ever, but obviously saddened. My mother took it very badly indeed, but, in the end, with my father's understanding both of her and of me, and his tactful help to us both, she came to the wedding and was generous in her good wishes.

Although many outstanding priests had resigned in the past few years and more were to follow, my leaving gave rise to a long correspondence in *The Tablet*. Dr Seymour Spencer and Father Francis Hastings summed up my position better that I could have done. The former wrote:

> Vatican 2 has, generally, liberated the relationship between priest and laity: the protective aloofness behind the *aura sanctitatis* has diminished. Intimate pastoral counselling has further diminished it; Park Place is an avowed pastoral centre at which pastoral counselling evidently focussed itself upon Father Faulkner (who, I believe, underwent special training for it). When he took his vow of celibacy could he have anticipated such exposure? May not priests so exceptionally exposed feel justifiably harassed under a rule of the Church, which, however sincerely originally avowed, yet effectively precludes them from a liaison in which we married counsellors find valuable protection against such exposure?

The latter ended his letter:

> I am no particular advocate of a married clergy. Married priests, 'tent-maker priests' – that is a different matter. In my

own parish there is a married deacon who is well respected. Were he to be ordained priest I can think of no inconveniences. Certainly a wife would prove more economic than a housekeeper . . . This letter has been evoked by the departure of an old friend from the ranks of the priesthood – Fr Anthony Faulkner. He was a good priest and would continue so to be, married or unmarried.

(*The Tablet*, 24 and 17 July 1976)

I might add that a secular priest does not take a vow of celibacy. It is a common misunderstanding. Celibacy is a canonical requirement for priestly ordination in the Catholic Church in the West, that is all. It is monks who vow poverty, chastity and obedience in order to live a dedicated life in a stable community which necessarily requires these commitments.

In a later chapter I shall write more about loss and gain. Here I only want to acknowledge that I was well aware of the sadness with which many people regarded my leaving. I had been through a painful and gradual liberation myself, but of course other people were not necessarily any different in their views of the priesthood from when they were in their formative years at school. They mostly refrained from writing to condemn, but the depth of their hurt became clear to me only recently when I asked an old parishioner and friend to say how she had viewed me as a priest and what she felt when I resigned. She said that at the time she had only seen my leaving as an act of tragic betrayal and treachery. She had been taught in her convent days that the priesthood was the highest calling open to man, that the priest was almost on another plane altogether from other men, that married people are expected by the Church to remain faithful to their vows and *a fortiori* priests should do the same. Now, all these years later, she has modified her views somewhat and is far more able to understand how both callings can become impossible for some people to remain in.

It says much for the charity of so many priests and people in the Church that, however dismayed they felt by my leaving, hardly any of them has spoken an unkind word to me about it. Indeed, whenever I have had occasion to meet old colleagues and parishioners I have met with warmth and affection. I have never for an instant regretted my resignation. Neither have I regretted the long years of training and priestly work that taught me so much about the constancy of God's love and the often heroic goodness of so many of his friends. I was now to meet these same qualities in a secular setting where again the spirit of God blows where it will and life is full of heroism.

3

MARRIAGE, FATHERHOOD
AND DIVORCE

I travelled hopefully and without fear into marriage, just as I had into the priesthood. There are men whose personalities are marked by maternal adoration and, as Freud remarked, the man who was the undisputed favourite of his mother walked through life like a God. I was not at all aware at the time that this was so, but subsequently came to realize it and suppose it was the source of self-confidence that, despite bad times, has not left me through life. Debbie and I married in August 1976, three months after my resignation. Originally alarmed, if not appalled, by the prospect of their daughter marrying an ex-priest nineteen years older than she, my parents-in-law were warm and supportive. The wedding was a most happy occasion. My family all came, except for my nun sister, and were equally generous in their good wishes. Numerous friends from our respective pasts came, among them a priest friend who told me frankly that he didn't know whether to laugh or cry but on balance thought he would laugh. My elder brother made me laugh; I had asked him to be best man and I was almost late for the wedding as a herd of cows in the lane by our cottage had delayed me. He said 'This is the last time I'm going to do this for you', looking at his watch at two minutes to twelve, with the bride and her father waiting beyond. Another difficulty was that I had hoped a Catholic priest could officiate with the Anglican priest who conducted the service, but the dispensation expected from Rome hadn't arrived in time. I suppose it said much for my attitude at the time that it really didn't seem to matter. On the other hand, when it did finally come we asked a priest friend to ratify the marriage according to Catholic Church law. I had a kind letter from the Catholic bishop of East Anglia on the occasion.

After a few weeks in the cottage, as we couldn't afford a honeymoon, Debbie started her teaching at a school near Beccles and I went off to Suffolk College in Ipswich for the social work course. They were wonderful years. I came to know and love the marshes around Minsmere, and to appreciate the atmosphere and architecture of Suffolk and Norfolk which I scarcely knew till then. The bracing air, vast skies, sparse population and utter unselfconsciousness of the local country people all combined to symbolize my own feelings of entering a new and different life, full of light, peace, directness and simplicity. The sheer normality of married life, with someone to leave in the morning and return to in the evening, brought vividly home to me how abnormal my life had been since I was sixteen. So did the ordinary domestic chores and budgeting, such as it was, which I had not had to do before. It was like rejoining the human race after a long absence. The other great change was the experience of earning a living in the usual way most people do; even going to college or to the practical placements while being funded to do so felt like real work, and indeed often was. Many priests, by no means all, work hard and for long hours, but living out a vocation while being supported financially by the parish or diocese is very different from having to deliver the goods in order to draw a grant or salary. Clergy in England, of most denominations, are a protected species whose material welfare is guaranteed, however much or little they contribute to the people they serve. I had not appreciated in any but a notional sense what it means to have to work from nine to five, five days a week, whether I wanted to or not. I hope I matured in those early years. Certainly I needed to.

Before leaving the ministry I had wondered how I would be perceived in a secular profession and how the reversion to being a student in adult life would feel after so many years in which I had been free to order days and weeks pretty much as I liked. In the event I found it stimulating and enjoyable. Many of the students were the same age as I, and had a common interest in and enthusiasm for the therapeutic dimension of the training and practice. It was a relief to be among people of like mind, and among equals. Consciously or not I had always accepted the attitude of Catholics towards their priests – one of deference, respect and affection.

These seemed to come (heaven help us!) as if by right. Now 'in the world' all of this would have to be earned – not that I had wasted much time in the past trying to earn deference. A friend brought all this home to me when we went to the wedding of one of her daughters. In the marquee she invited me to dance, and when we left she traced the cross on my forehead. 'I couldn't have danced with you or blessed you before', she laughed.

As the training came to an end Debbie and I awaited our first baby. She had read as much as possible about what to expect and how to handle the process. She was not a surgeon's daughter for nothing. I think it was early in the morning that she asked me to ring the hospital. I too had done a spot of reading about how to help, and took literally the advice to have a good meal before setting off as there might be a long labour ahead. Outwardly we seemed calm as we drove the twenty-five miles or so. We would not have been so relaxed if we had known that the labour would be very long and painful. I shall never forget the look of bliss and exhaustion in mother and baby when at last Rose was born. It was midnight and, after a fond farewell, I drove to my parents-in-law near whom we lived and celebrated their first grandchild with champagne. I was in a kind of euphoria and rather spoilt things by driving on at four in the morning to an old friend who had retired to a neighbouring cottage. We celebrated, this time with malt whisky – a mixture not to be recommended.

Rose was and is our pride and joy. So are the two boys, Tom and Joe, who were born in the next three and a half years. One curious effect on me, which I haven't heard others mention though no doubt it is common enough, is that after Rose was born I no longer felt afraid of my own death. Marriage, work and parenthood gave me a sense of being whole, of being human and alive. All the years of spiritual and religious works, the love of God, the fatherhood implied in the ministry, had failed to do for me what these natural areas of fulfilment seemed to do abundantly. Maybe I had been in the wrong vocation all that time, or maybe it is a familiar example of the old saying that grace builds on nature. God does not normally bring about by directly spiritual means what he has intended the natural order to achieve.

The next two years were a compound of both Debbie and myself trying to rearrange ourselves now that we were parents. I think I failed to give proper consideration to the change in her that it brought about. Looking back, I also think I took mothering too much for granted and did not understand how exhausting it can be. At the same time I was coping with a variety of new and difficult problems at work. The boss was a gifted and shrewd man, but he was also liable to extremes of elation and alarm. I used to come home tired not so much by what I had done all day but by what might have happened all day. Social work is to do with high levels of risk: will that father beat up his wife or children? Should a suspicion of child abuse be pursued or is it safer to offer support? Should an old person, mentally disordered but fearful of being taken away, be left at home with the attendant dangers of self-harm or neglect, or placed safely in a home or hospital? It is also to do with loss: we are dealing all the time with adults and children, the very old and the very young who have lost their independence, their health, their partner, their self-esteem, their job. In the past I had been able to offer the consolations of religion, which are sometimes derided but which are very real. Now I was working with disadvantaged people whose life was in a mess, and had to try and help them find practical ways of coping without any reference to help from above. I will say more about all this in another chapter and here only want to observe that I was so occupied with helping other people that I was probably less supportive than I should have been at home.

I think I lost my equilibrium in all this readjustment for both Debbie and me. We apparently presented as a warm and loving household, to judge from the numbers of friends who loved to come and stay or who asked us to stay with them. Debbie's old and new friends and mine enriched our lives greatly and we had a huge sense of joy in Rose's development. But probably we were, like so many new parents, too stretched to be able to take enough real care of one another and make the time to talk. Despite my own counselling experience, our backgrounds made the expression of true feelings difficult, the dangerous feelings that include anger and adoration and disappointment and frustration, and I suppose we both kept them down and turned our attention outwards to being parents and entertaining friends. I was brought up short when we talked about having a second child and Debbie intimated that it would help her to feel more settled as a family if we had two close together. We should have looked at what that remark implied, but did not. Perhaps we were both somewhat afraid of looking too closely at our mutual disappointment. On the other hand there was so much that was so good – we shared a sense of humour, the same perspective on children, we enjoyed each other's friends, we loved going to church, Anglican or Catholic, together.

Tom was born two years after Rose. By comparison his was a fairly easy birth and we were of course thrilled by his arrival. His coming into the world as another great gift was overshadowed for me by the death of my mother. Not very long after we married, my nun sister had died of cancer at fifty years of age. She and my mother were very close to each other in many ways, and I have felt ever since that her death and my departure from the priesthood had some part to play in my mother developing cancer at about the same time. Both she and my father suffered intensely and it was a sort of terrible relief when she died. She never complained, though she enduring every indignity and pain possible. I felt, however, that I was part of her unhappiness, because beneath her outward acceptance of my change in life she had really not come to terms with it at all. There was nothing I could do or say that would make any difference, but I felt that her affection had been decisively withdrawn and that I could be of no comfort to her in the most painful days. I had been to see her earlier in her illness, only to hear her say bitterly that I had been lovely, once. Debbie too had withdrawn her affection and I felt alone in sorrow.

Almost immediately after Tom's birth we moved from Minsmere to the north of Suffolk close to Diss where much of my work lay. Suffolk on the border of Norfolk is very different from the east coast near Aldeburgh, Walberswick and Southwold. For sea, avocets and sailing, Snape Maltings, weekend homes and green wellies substitute black boots and sugar beet, cornfields and, on the whole, an indigenous population who had been there for generations. Diss is a few miles away and at the time was a small town where the economy was about to boom and property was rising in value. It has a rich variety of interconnected families. The country people are friendly, kind and taciturn, with a highly developed sense of humour. Many of the villages have a pre-Reformation wool church that in any other county might be mistaken for a cathedral.

The next change in my fortunes was that just after we moved and Tom was tiny, my boss offered me the job I had originally sought two years before. I had been travelling fifty or seventy miles to work each day, and during the heavy snows of the late seventies these were hazardous and nerve-wracking miles across small country roads that were never cleared. Now I was to be based in the health centre in Diss, just six miles away. It would allow a freedom to work as I liked, provided it all got done, in a most agreeable setting. The actual building is in the former grounds of the manor house across the road, in one of the prettiest town streets in England, according to John Betjeman. I accepted at once. It made sense to me that a social worker should be based alongside health professionals right in the community, accessible, locally accountable, known personally in the town and surroundings. It is the only such arrangement in Norfolk, and is still relatively uncommon anywhere. I can't think why, because it works so well. I particularly love strolling through the market on a Friday and meeting people. 'I'm so glad I saw you, you're just the person I wanted to talk to.' 'Could you come and see my mother, she's very confused.' A lot of work gets done while I look for bargains among the bric-à-brac and occasionally come up with a find. One such is a little clock, 1950s. It cost £5, an extra £18 to get it going, and is worth at least £200.

I would like to look at other dimensions in my life at that time. First, the spiritual life, for want of a better description (as I do not think it can be in any way separated from life itself): on one level it was as before. I kept in touch with old friends, priest and nun friends among them. We would continue to talk about the way the Church was going under the increasingly conservative and in some ways regressive papacy of John Paul II. But at a deeper level I had for the time being lost the tranquillity and ability to pray in silence for sustained lengths of time. This lack was partly counterbalanced by the discovery that in Stowmarket, sixteen miles away, there had arrived an old friend who was a Benedictine monk from Quarr Abbey. He was originally invited to be parish priest there while the incumbent took a sabbatical to take stock, but in the event he stayed there ten years. Fr James and I (and indeed the children) have spent much time together and in his gentle, wholly unselfconscious way he has helped me as much as anybody to regain a sense of integrity and optimism. Later, as I shall describe, I returned to the practice of prayer. For the meantime, weekly mass at Stowmarket was a support and an outlet, and an attractive face of Catholicism for the small children to grow up with.

Secondly, there are the various friends who have enriched my life so much and who continue to do so. Soon after marrying, I contacted Hubert Richards who now lived in Norwich. As I mentioned in chapter 2, he had been a priest and Scripture scholar, first at the Westminster seminary and later at Corpus Christi College in Bayswater. He was now married to Clare, formerly a nun, and at about the time Rose was one year old they adopted twins from Colombia. In addition to numerous fun days with their children and ours, they have welcomed me to lunch once a week for the past fourteen years. We have spent much of the time, by no means all, debriefing on our past. Although we feel happy where we are now, he and his wife teaching and writing on scriptural and other religious matters, I doing pastoral, counselling work to some extent as before, we also feel the need to go over the past in various ways both sad and glad. Their example and encouragement and affection have probably helped me through difficult times as much as anything has. We also laugh like drains and exchange ideas and books. Bert loves Hasidic (Jewish) stories. Like Jesus, he answers a question by asking a question or telling a story. In his company I wonder how little the difference is between Catholicism and Judaism, apart from the timing of the Messiah. Another staunch friend is Barbara Coventry. She is a retired GP who was once a parishioner in Fareham and who came to live near us in Minsmere. Her Jesuit cousin John was a theological mentor to me when I was at Park Place. She has been a most supportive friend in every way over the last twenty-five years. She is an original. I was writing an essay on the virginal conception and asked her whether she believed in the doctrine. 'No, never have,' was her reply. Yet she goes and works for weeks on end in Lourdes every year, helping the sick and dying. I feel sure that religion is, in the end, more about what one does than what one thinks one believes.

In many ways life was very good to me, but I became painfully aware that Debbie was not happy. During her third pregnancy we began to go to a marriage guidance counsellor every fortnight. This was painful, but it did give us the safe opportunity to discuss some of the problems we were experiencing. It became clear that we simply did not perceive our marriage in the same light. Joe was born shortly after the sessions finished, with our problems unresolved. His birth was relatively easy for Debbie and himself, as if he were born considerate and determined not to be hard work.

He certainly hasn't been that since. A year later, things between Debbie and me had not improved and she told me that she no longer felt able to continue in the marriage, that we must separate. For another agonizing year we stayed uncomfortably in the same cottage, so near but, oh, so far. We formally separated when Joe was nearly two. Here again the observations of Goethe quoted above proved true. All sorts of things occurred to help us that would never otherwise have occurred. Almost as soon as we put the cottage on the market we found a ready buyer determined to have it at a good price. Debbie bought a cottage six miles away in which she was to live for some years with the children. I was anxious not to change more than could be avoided, and by good fortune secured a cottage just three doors down the lane where we had lived for the past four years. After I had made an offer on it, another prospective buyer increased the offer. However, the sister of the owner lived in the same lane and knew my circumstances. She stoutly said that she wanted me to have it and wasn't into contract races. The actual move, though sad enough, went smoothly. Friends helped Debbie with her move one day and the next day turned up with carts and barrows and wheeled all the remaining furniture to my new cottage. My younger brother Brian came up from Wiltshire to help, and between them they did everything. We had lunch and drinks in the village pub afterwards, and in the evening they all came back for port and sandwiches. Some of those who helped cart the heavy beds and tables I hardly knew at all, just friendly village people. They even ran up some makeshift curtains which I have only just replaced nine years later.

Moving day was 25 March. It was very cold in the new cottage which hadn't been lived in for three years since the death of the old lady who had owned it. I wasn't alarmed by the damp: studs, timbers and thatch don't last for 350 years and suddenly collapse, and the builder had also assured me that woodworm was not a danger. The oak studs and rafters are like cast iron and the worm cannot penetrate far. But for months I felt daunted by the cold bedroom with its exposed beams and large empty bed, and the total, almost eery silence of the dark evenings and nights. It wasn't just the loss of a personal relationship that had seemed so full of bright promise, it was also the loss of family life and my inability to do anything about it that hurt so much. I felt emotionally choked, and indeed did choke badly on the way to mass one Sunday. The poor children in the back thought I was going to pass out, and so did I. I foolishly didn't take any time off work to recover some sort of balance, and was therefore bothered and undermined by a series of illnesses for weeks afterwards.

The loss of family life was mercifully not complete. We had arranged amicably that the children, now aged six, four and two, should be with their mother from Monday to Friday and with me for the weekends. I used to meet them from school or home after work and return them to their home on Monday morning. This provided the abiding advantage that as parents we could exchange news and views as and when the need arose and that the children saw us as a partnership as far as welfare and upbringing were concerned. This has proved invaluable over the years, and has also allowed both parents to express gratitude and appreciation to each other for their mutual care for the children.

Weekends have been and are still pivotal for me. At first, and for a long time, I both looked forward to them but also feared the long evenings after the children had gone to bed. Because I was fifty at the time of the move I would be pretty tired at the end of the day and not inclined to do anything very creative. I felt the loneliness acutely. Of course I was aware that it was pure fantasy to imagine that all tired parents could sink back and bask in each other's company in the evening. But it is a powerful fantasy all the same, and numerous single parents I have talked to share it: every week-end, every holiday, the world is full of happily married couples with their children and single parents are – alone. It has taken years for this haunting imagination to disappear from me, and of course even when I felt it most acutely there were also happy times when friends would come and stay, or occasionally we would go off and visit one of my family. The problem, then as now, is that my brothers and sister live the other side of the country, as do the children's cousins on my side of the family. Fortunately for them, they are able more easily to see relatives on their mother's side who mostly live in East Anglia.

It seems to me that there are advantages and disadvantages in being a lone, part-time parent. The latter are really too obvious to point out: the lack of role models where parents remain alone, and the assimilation of a second father or mother figure if they remarry. This can cause great difficulties for the natural parent and for the children, as every social worker, doctor, priest and lawyer is well aware. In my children's case the disadvantages seem to have been minimized by the consistency of our original arrangements for them, and the fact that their mother remained alone for six years before marrying again. I may say that her new husband is very good with and to the children and has always been exceptionally pleasant towards me. The other obvious disadvantage is the restlessness sometimes felt by all concerned, in both households, occasioned by the weekly move from one to the other. A weekend visit will sometimes involve a car boot full of clothes and toys, homework and musical instruments. Again, this is such a long-standing routine that the children seem to have coped with it very well indeed. I often think they have managed it all far better than I, and would like to let them speak for themselves. I asked them if they would write down how they see their dad, to help me with this chapter. This is what they wrote, unaltered:

Rose: When I was six years old my parents split up. I didn't really know what was going on, except that from then on we would have two homes, one where mum lived and one for dad. Life must have got better from then in a funny kind of way. What I didn't realize was that both my parents must have been going through hell. Dad moved a couple of doors down the lane, into a cottage that is now embedded with memories, happy and sad. A dedicated Catholic family, we regularly attended church, which is what I think kept dad together. He made new friends and slowly started to pull his life together. As well as doing all this, he learnt how to be the best father ever. I will always remember when I was small, every Friday when we came to visit dad for the weekend, he would always cook spaghetti whether it was winter or summer. Then one day, in the winter, when the lane was coated with ice and snow, dad took my younger brother and me outside so we could skate. Tom was holding on to one of dad's hands and I was holding on to the other. Suddenly he fell down, he kept hold of us so that we weren't hurt but as we lay on the ice I thought, just to myself, that something was wrong. Dad got up, slowly and carefully, and got us inside. We were fine, just a few bruises, but dad couldn't breathe properly. A friend who was staying with us phoned an ambulance and dad was whisked off. He returned with two broken ribs. He still looked after us though, he made sure we had everything we needed. Dad's best point is that he is so generous and puts other people first. However dad has one bad point that I can think of, he can be a little impatient. This kind of contradicts what I have just said but I can't find any other words to describe it. He is also kind, loving, reliable, funny, and if he ever gets angry it is never for long. I think that being a priest has put a positive experience on his life and I think that he is a very special person and my brothers and I are the luckiest people in the world to have him as a father.

Tom: I see dad as a very loving kind man who would stop at nothing to please us. He is very generous and loves giving us treats and presents. He is always there whenever we or anyone else for that matter needs him.

I love mending things so I am never short of things to do as dad is always breaking things. He has a good sense of humour and once I nearly laughed at one of his jokes. As a dedicated crossword man, dad has a very good vocabulary. He sometimes gets cross but never more than ten minutes. Dad does have many friends, but I often worry about him during the week. He is a very indoor person and unlike me loves a game of cribbage with a gin and tonic. We often play card games with him in the evening. I've never seen him watch the TV for more than fifty minutes. Dad is a warm, kind, loving man and I never want to lose him.

Joe: I see my dad as a brave, trustworthy and forgiving man. He obviously finds weeks difficult as he has nobody to talk to in the long, cold winter evenings. He must find it especially hard on Mondays, after a jolly weekend, coming home to a sad empty cottage. I think I am the richest boy on Earth although, literally, I'm not. In the world's eyes my father may not be more than a joke but in my eyes he is the greatest hero that ever there was, his sense of humour combined with his forever lovingness makes him wonderful to live with.

The fact that Dad used to be a priest certainly affects us, for, like the Lord, whatever we do we are always forgiven as long as we are truly sorry. Dad is not bighead or a bad loser. He can take powerful blows without taking it out on anyone else. He has never forced me to do anything, in fact he is the only person who hasn't, and never will, that is another thing that makes him so fabulous. I have often heard him say 'what is mine is yours'. This is a tiny fraction of his ongoing generosity. He has no bad spots that I can think of here and now.

I have quoted these notes here in full, at the risk of sounding self-satisfied, because of the light they throw on the children's own generous and lovely nature. They are now fifteen, thirteen and eleven years old. I am not dreading their teens as parents keep telling me I should. Tom's notes remind me – and I promise this is the only anecdote I shall offer, as usually one's children's sayings are as boring as other people's holiday snaps – of the evening when they were first in the cottage and were camping down on the floor of my bedroom as they said they were scared of their own. Rose wanted to get up. She told Tom to mind out as she might tread on him. He said she mustn't tread on him because God was in him and she'd be treading on God. Rose replied that God wasn't a body that could be hurt. Tom agreed: 'No, he's just a heart and a spirit.' I sometimes think the children are too.

A great advantage is that I have had no option but to become involved in and close to the three of them in a way I could have so easily avoided in marriage. Washing and ironing, making beds and tidying, playing monopoly and taking them to the sea, camping and other holidays together have inevitably brought us close to one another. So has cooking. I try to avoid convenience foods so we eat simply and well. From watching both parents cook, and learning it at school, each of them can now prepare a meal and Rose has learnt to make delicious cakes and puddings with the help of old cookery books.

Children of a lone parent seem to have an especially strong bond with one another, and mine certainly play a good deal together. I have never known them to quarrel. Perhaps they are able to feel relaxed because there is no united parental front lined up against them. And they do not need to play one parent off against another.

One misgiving I do have where they are concerned is that they do not know me as a man relating to a woman. Rose seems to have no memory of the time I was married to her mother, and a profound relationship I have had for years has not reached a point where we can be fully united and together. What they do know and see are my deep friendships with both men and women, so at least the ready display of affection and physical embraces are nothing new to them.

I realize that I am most fortunate in having such easy and appreciative children, and that for many lone parents it is a difficult road, perhaps especially for mothers. Where there is an absent or non-caring father, sons often become unruly or worse and daughters may be more likely to become lone parents themselves, often at an early age. I also realize that many such parents do not have a co-operative ex-partner, a house of their own, a car, a salaried job and a range of supportive networks. I realize too that, through no virtue of my own, having children at the age of forty-four and more instead of the more usual twenty-four, I had worked out many of the major conflicts to do with self-identity, self-confidence and self-value, and so was not in danger of projecting all kinds of guilt and anxiety on to them.

I said earlier that I would return to the matter of my prayer life. This was in abeyance all through the separation and for four years after that. I prayed, but only to say prayers. The more contemplative kind of prayer seemed impossible because of the emotional turmoil that made sitting still so difficult. I could offer a kind of dumb agony to God and ask not to be bitter. The psychological pain arose from several sources. I could not really understand why the marriage had failed. I could not offer any kind of help to Debbie either. Nor could I accept the bleak possibility of remaining alone indefinitely, without a companion or lover. It then occurred to me that the underlying problem was that I was still inwardly denying that the marriage was irretrievably over. We were not formally divorced for years, and I had by no means let go of the hope of a reconciliation. So I sought out a counsellor and looked at all this in depth. It was difficult for both the counsellor and myself. We were both professionals known to one another, doing the same kind of work; I was aware that her method was very skilful, she was aware that I was aware, and so on. But the sessions made all the difference to my state of mind. Quite simply they enabled me to accept the death of the marriage and bury it. I don't think I could have done that without the sessions, just four of them, one a week. The relief was so great that, although I did not exactly feel whole and well again, at least I did feel. It was like being able to breathe again, to see and touch and hear in a way I had been unable to for so long.

With this liberation I sat up in bed one morning, very early, and let God's presence envelop me again. I could only bear it for half an hour or so, but it was a turning point in my life and I have continued with this silent prayer practically every day since then. It is not the prayer of words, images, texts; it is more like a heaving up of the heart and will in silence. There was and is, however, an underlying if unspoken prayer of petition that God would show me the way ahead. I was travelling again, but I didn't know where. What should I be and do with the rest of my life? What vocation did I have now that I had left the priesthood and my marriage had failed? I will attempt some sort of deeper look at the whole question of vocation later. What I want to dwell on in the next chapter is the central issue for me and so many people – the process of bereavement and healing, of loss and gain.

4

LOSS AND GAIN, SUFFERING AND GROWTH

May I open this chapter with a disclaimer? Whatever I have suffered over the years, and I have left out a good deal in order to protect other people, is nothing compared to the suffering we see daily on the television screen in the Sudan, Somalia, Bosnia. It is nothing to what I have witnessed in so many people past and present. It does not compare with the experience of a former parishioner whom I met again recently after thirty years and who wrote as follows:

> I was delighted to find you are one of the speakers on the course . . . I had always been interested in the Benedictine life and, after guidance(?) I entered. This was to be the wrong place for me, but I did not worry as it was great to be serving God, singing daily mass and divine office, making vestments and so on. I was looking forward to becoming a fully professed nun.
>
> On the day I was to make my first vows, I was called to the abbess who made me leave at once, with no chance to inform my mother or make any arrangements. She had discovered that I was born out of wedlock and the nuns agreed you can't have 'bad blood' in a convent and I was the 'rotten fruit of an illicit union'. When I got home my old grandmother said to me 'O God, Harry's bastard, I thought we'd got rid of her for life'. I went to the parish priest for help. He said: 'Well now, m'dear, you came into the world an unwanted bastard, so you'll go through it and out the other end the same way. If your own family don't want you, you can't expect anyone else

to.' His words and those of the abbess and my grandmother have been with me ever since . . . Now, after many terrible experiences, job loss, homelessness, bereavement, poverty, ill health − I am scratching along on the basic O.A.P. and am quite alone in the world.

Neither does my own share of difficulty compare with the kind of suffering I hear of anonymously from social-work colleagues, especially in child guidance. I can only say that I write about what I know, and that my own suffering has felt acute, almost overwhelming to me, whatever it may look like to others.

I remember one evening, about a year after the marriage breakdown, that it was cold. I cannot bear being cold and I was miserable. After a long day's work I felt, as usual, alone. So I rang a favourite relation who asked 'How are you?' 'Bloody awful,' I replied. He said, 'No you're not, you've got a nice cottage, lovely children . . .'. It makes me angry when other people deny the feelings I know I have. Often these people cannot own their own. English middle-class people seem hell-bent on denying their feelings. Why can't we face them? Why do we suppress so much? Why can't we cry out, make fools of ourselves, come clean and be real, truthful? What can we lose?

Denial is the obvious first reaction to pain that cannot be borne. I hurt, therefore I deny I hurt, therefore I do not hurt. So much neurosis, which for me means useless displacement of activity leading to weariness and frustration, arises from a refusal to accept ourselves as we are. 'It is expected of me that . . . I should . . . I must . . . I ought . . . I'll be in trouble if I don't' − perhaps these are not the unwritten scripts of today's children but they were when I was a child.

I see denial all around me. That the marriage is over. That my religious life is finished. That my hope is dead. That my friend is hurting. That my congregation is bored stiff. That the choir is rotten. That the legal system is unreliable and helpless. That the doctor doesn't care. We go on hoping and pretending. We need to, perhaps. But surely we need just as must to be clear about what we are denying so that we can construct a better way.

Denial is the first defence against shock of a serious kind. It gives a space in which we can gather resources and gradually absorb the impact. As human beings cannot bear very much reality, we filter the sewage that comes our way. We may take in the awful news at an intellectual level yet not absorb it at all. We are not pure intellect: we have to take in through the heart, emotions and guts as well as through the mind. The ancients placed the seat of thinking in the heart and of emotions in the bowels – one storey down from our location of them. A client of mine was with her husband in a terrible car crash in which he was reduced to a red pulp and she remained conscious and physically intact. She suffered a double trauma, the impact both of the crash and of the loss. Months afterwards she told me that she was waiting for her husband to put up the new curtains which were too heavy for her to lift. She had assimilated his death at a notional level only, even though she had been to the funeral, wept for weeks and talked for many hours to me about it.

It is costly to take in the reality of loss. I am aware that I denied my own hidden desire to leave the priesthood for many years, while my actions belied my implicit professions of fidelity. In the same way I had many intimations of the death of my marriage but I did not allow them into my heart or deeper feelings. I intellectualized them, thinking that if I were faithful and persevering nothing need change. And recently a man of about seventy who had been coming to a group for years talked haltingly for the first time of his suppressed grief. What had stirred his emotion was the anniversary of the opening of a local airfield, which he had worked on in 1942. This had reminded him that when he was forty-two himself he had lost his only son, aged two. He, the father, was laid up in bed and awaiting an operation on his back. His wife came to him in distress and said their son was missing. He raised himself and went with her to search. They found their son drowned in a water butt, the soles of his shoes upturned on the surface of the water. The sweet peas his son had brought his father two days before were laid now on the child's coffin a few days afterwards. He could not talk about it with his wife and, during the months in hospital soon after, nobody adverted to his loss: he was a 'back problem', not a human being with far greater distress. His wife left him and he told nobody how he was feeling about the double loss. Now, thirty years later, he is still incapacitated from Christmas until June, reliving the Christmases they should have had, the birthdays, the anniversary of the death. He was denied expression of grief at the time and mourns, unhealed, still.

Denial brings costly consequences. Until very recently it has been widely practised by professionals: miscarriages were disposed of without counselling or ceremony; newborn babies that died were not seen by the mother and she was given no help to mourn physically or emotionally; children were not allowed to go to funerals of loved ones; patients were not told they were dying. When I was at college and a colleague left, nothing was said. It was as if he had never existed. Nobody worried about the feelings of other students who knew and loved him and didn't blame him for leaving – the fellow had somehow failed and nothing must be said. Nurses wept in the sluice over the death of a young patient, with no help from the sister because they were all supposed to be professionally detached. They broke their hearts at seeing children tied to bedposts, frantic for their mothers who weren't allowed to stay. Feelings were denied, denied. The psychological damage was severe, and to this day many therapists are trying to help old men and women who were in some way abused in their young years and never allowed to say what they felt. Symptoms never go away until the cause has been faced, expressed and talked through.

I spend much of my professional, and indeed private life trying to encourage the expression of feeling in suffering clients and friends. This evening I watched a programme about a therapist taking a mother through the trauma of coming to terms with the death of her newborn. The baby was beautifully dressed and placed in a tiny Moses basket. The mother, father and young sister were able gradually to hold and stroke her, and watch the therapist take hand- and foot-prints which they would keep. The effect on them was extremely moving. The mother had already suffered two miscarriages without any such help and was now assured that immediate and expressed grief would save her from long-term ill effects.

I have come to loathe the spurious comment that time heals. In itself, time heals nothing. The acute agony of bereavement does not last more than a year or two, though waves of pain still break through, released by a painful memory or a pang of regret. But a dull, aching void will take its place and, if the bereavement brought a sense of guilt or shame because of what the bereaved felt he or she had done or should have done, the emotion will not go away. Feelings are like electrical charges. They are either dispersed or channelled. If neither happens they break out in some sort of psychosomatic symptom or psychiatric distress. It is no coincidence that Fr Harry Williams writes in his autobiography *Some Day I'll Find You* that the reliving of his memories brought on psoriasis. It has done the same for me in writing these chapters. It only affects me where it can't be seen, not on the face and hands. Much unresolved pain is like that, suffered without others being aware of it. A small example, to offset the major trauma of the father mentioned earlier, was given me by an aunt who is now eighty-five years old. I wanted her to give me some idea of the world into which my mother had been born, so I wrote inviting her to say how she felt when she herself was about nine. She remembered very little, but two matters stuck in her mind. She had spent much of her life as a convent schoolgirl sitting in the corridor in disgrace because of some bright remark she made in class that was taken as rudeness. The coldness of the nuns' response re-affirmed the coldness of her own parents who gave her no hugs, no expressed affection. As a result she has gone through life 'hard on the outside, soft as putty on the inside'. She also remembers being sent to her room in disgrace because of something her sister had actually done and not owned up to. She has not forgotten the look of triumph on her sister's face as she went upstairs. Seventy-six years later it still rankles.

When denial following trauma is no longer possible, we often begin to react with anger. To be bereft is to be robbed, with consequent feelings of outrage: 'Why me? what have I done to deserve this?' When my wife told me she was seeing another man, I wanted to kill him. I thought of schemes to do so but couldn't find one that would not implicate me. I am sure I could not really have emptied out his brake fluid, but I wanted to. When I saw him with my wife and small children one day while I was at work, I wanted to open the car window and shout at him or accelerate and knock him down, but of course I didn't. Instead I suffered terrible palpitations, sleeplessness and all the rest.

It is difficult to express anger in a helpful way. Aristotle recog-nized this: 'Any fool can fly into a passion. But to be angry with the right person to the right extent and at the right time and with the right object and in a right way – that is not easy and not everyone can do it.' Many of us who cannot do it will suppress anger and suffer in various ways. We may displace it on to God and give up what we thought was our faith but what was really a kind of conditional love. We may displace it on to other people we choose to blame – the driver of the car, the doctor, the nurse, the social worker or whoever we think failed us. Or we load it on to close friends and relations who will tend thereafter to leave us alone and so drive us into further isolation and more anger.

I wonder why it is so difficult to express anger accurately? In my case I think it is to do with the attendant feeling of shame. I see angry people as shameful and am ashamed when I get angry. Somewhere in childhood I have learnt that to be angry is disgraceful. It is very inhibiting indeed, because it forces me to present as calm when I am in turmoil within. Sometimes I use my command of language to say something clever and cutting at a safe distance from the person I am angry with.

The really corrosive effect of suppressed anger is that we turn it against ourselves instead of directing it accurately. This leads to a feeling of impotence and depression. But why should I feel guilty because other people have hurt me, messed me about, misused my good intentions?

Depression is either 'clinical', in which case there are alarming symptoms such as sleeplessness, loss of appetite and of any desire for food, company, conversation, work, sexual pleasure, prayer or any other of life's joys. Or it is a less obvious feeling of sadness and despair, coupled with a weight that can feel overwhelming. I walked in mud for years after the end of my marriage, enjoying little, barely alive, somewhat like Samuel Johnson who wrote of his bereavement: 'I have ever since seemed to myself broken off from mankind, a kind of solitary wanderer in the wild of life, without any direction, or fixed point of view: a gloomy gazer on the world to which I have little relation' (written in 1755 on the loss of his wife).

Those years of heaviness were also, I think, years of silent growth. I have said *ad nauseam* that during much of my life I have felt lonely, but I had never had actually to live alone in a house. At first I was anxious and fearful, locking doors and leaving lights on all night. I also felt unreal. Johnson also commented that marriage may have many trials but celibacy has no pleasures. Celibacy was the least unbearable part of it. Far worse was the endless experience of having to carry myself the whole time, to learn to be complete within myself, to laugh or weep alone, think of what to shop for, make time to buy it, bring it home, cook it and then dine alone. I made a point of keeping up appearances even to myself because

I instinctively knew how easy it would be to slip into self-neglect. So I would polish the table and the silver, starch the linen, lay the table properly, open the wine and enjoy the meal. I would light the fire every evening and cocoon myself in the little heavily beamed sitting-room. To friends I appeared to have become rather a donnish figure, alone with books, music, fire, pipe and wine. They did not know that I was simply trying to survive and hold on to some self-respect. The silent growth came through my being forced to face myself and the reality about myself. In the evenings the silence is total, and if there is nothing that appeals on Radio 3 I sink into the silence. After a time the fearfulness passed, but I would warn anyone who has not been bereaved that grief and fear feel very much the same.

As feeling of any kind was damped down, prayer too was of no consolation. I tried to heave this state of helplessness up to heaven with my will, and obscurely felt at one with suffering humanity. Very deep down, and inaccessible for years to come, there was peace and joy and resignation. At least I hurt, so I knew I was alive. Gibran wrote that the greater the sorrow that carves into our being, the greater the joy it can contain. I also became very sensitive to the children and to their need for affection and attention. They certainly received both from their mother during the week, and I made very sure they would at weekends as well. Sadness did not prevent us from hooting with laughter on the little steam trains at Bressingham or from enjoying holidays together and playing card games hour after hour. I also discovered that I could hold them spellbound by making up stories as they were going to sleep.

A friend of thirty years' standing exemplifies better than I the possibilities for growth even in terrible pain and depression. I first met her when I was a curate and she was about sixteen. She presented herself after mass one day and said she couldn't believe in God any more. She had been more or less abandoned by her parents and brought up by an aunt in Vienna, but had now returned to her parents in England. I was able to help her perceive that she could hardly feel confidence in a heavenly Father if she had no experience of a reliable human father. Giving her 'permission' not to believe in God paradoxically helped her to believe again, or at least to feel loved by God. Perhaps my love for her was some kind of vehicle for this greater love. We met again when she was at university and have kept in touch ever since. I officiated at her wedding in due course, after she had twice fallen in love and lost both fiancés in road accidents. Her marriage was a disaster: her husband was so cruel to the two boys that one of them had to be taken into care. Eventually she read law and was called to the bar, by which time she felt financially secure enough to divorce and cope on her own. Her elder son went abroad and her younger son, who at sixteen looked identical to his mother at that age, did well at school and started at university. His mother did not remarry although for years she had longed to. She adored her son and he was indeed a lovable boy, open, generous, kind, thoughtful and unselfish. On his way back to university one night he was killed in a car crash. His mother was distraught in the extreme and I thought she would die of grief. Yet in these terrible last years she has rediscovered the reality of God's love in a most authentic way. This is what she wrote to me recently:

> I think the spirit of God works exceedingly hard but has a difficult time actually getting through. People are so taken up by what they get out of something, many of them don't get within a million miles of ever giving unconditional love to any creature. Even when people say they love somebody, and love their work etc. they still often insist that the people they love behave in a particular way and that the work goes in a particular direction. This isn't love at all, I think it's bullying and we're all guilty of it.
>
> I believe that God is interested more than anything else in our efforts to learn what love is. My own most recognizable brief instants of understanding something about unconditional love and compassion relate to my dog. I once stood looking at him curled up asleep on the sofa. He looked so old and unspeakably vulnerable and I felt what a great responsibility it is to have such power over another defenceless creature. And then I felt that God's relationship to us has similarities with my power over Sam. We don't truly understand how much love and compassion God has for us, any more than Sam understands what I feel for him. Also there is nothing Sam can give me that I need – except his love. It is exactly the same with us and God. He doesn't need anything from us either, but it gives him the greatest pleasure if we manage a few little instances of true love for him.

People always seem to be praying for benefits in this world. You may know a better class of people than I do, in this respect! They always want themselves and those they love to be reprieved from illnesses and so on. Yet I see the spirit of God most obviously at work successfully when people grow and improve as the result of going through some disasters. What we should pray for, I think, is to be given the courage and whatever else it takes, to use painful experiences for our own personal growth.

I mention this because it is one area I think where priests, amongst other people, go dreadfully wrong. They fail to teach others what disasters in life are really for. Instead they keep the idea going that we should pray to God for sweeties in this life only. You probably know dozens of priests who are not like that at all, but as it happens I don't!

Our ability to use suffering creatively and grow by it will be influenced by earlier important life events. We are born losers. Birth brings the loss of life within the womb. If one imagines talking to a baby a few days before birth and asking whether he would like to leave his warm, dark, safe home where he is fed without effort, bathes in lovely fluid and is as close as possible to his mother – asking, too, whether he would care to make a painful journey and be squeezed through a narrow channel while his mother cries in pain – the baby would no doubt reply that he would prefer to stay where he is. Yet, if the mothering is good enough, the baby will soon learn the joy of being at the breast, of discovering its independent existence, of being held and adored and smiled upon, of being able to laugh and gurgle. The world becomes a most interesting and exciting place, and a return to a womblike existence unthinkable. What at the time seemed loss has now become gain. The same sort of process will be repeated with weaning. What baby wants to leave the loving breast? If the weaning is handled sensitively the baby will in fact learn to appreciate a wider variety of food and drink, and the associated pleasures of choice, handling food, throwing it on the floor, stirring it about. It is interesting in this connection that French mothers give bits of whatever is on their plate to the small child, so developing its palate to savour strong and varied flavours. We English tend to give children boring pap, which is perhaps why our palates are uneducated and we continue to eat boring, bland food when we are adults.

Loss and gain are experienced again when the child first leaves the mother and goes to play school, later to school proper. He or she loses the special place at home, the undivided attention of the parent, and has to compete in a room full of other children where none is special. If the schools are good enough the child will eventually be glad to have been introduced to a wider world where the joys of learning and friendship will amply compensate for the loss. All subsequent life events will follow the pattern laid down in these years. If by the age of two or three the child has learnt a basic trust in the mother and in himself or herself as a valued and dear human being, if the experiences of loss have proved to bring greater benefits, then all future major changes will be viewed with a sense of optimism and confidence because change in the past has usually been rewarding. How else could young people find the courage to leave home altogether for college or other employment, or abandon father and mother to cling to a spouse instead? Marriage is a loss – not many partners can be expected to give the unconditional love and care that a mother gives. But, of course, it is also an immense gain if the relationship is a good one. Middle age too will bring the loss of youth, fertility, ambitious hopes of promotion. It can also bring great joys: self-assurance, equanimity, the freedom to travel and take up new interests once the children have become independent. When I was forty I resolved that I would never worry again. In fact I certainly have, but at least I have only worried when there was good cause. I no longer worried about being myself. I found comfort and challenge in the expression that by the time we are forty we have the face we deserve. Life may treat us hard but we still have some freedom to smile even if we don't much feel like it, and the smile on the face will usually bring a lift to the heart.

I suppose all loss is a kind of rehearsal for the final loss of independence, health and life itself. If my experience of life has been that change usually brings new possibilities and fulfilment, I hope I shall look upon death in the same light. I wonder what sort of childhood the writer of 'Abide with me' had, that he should complain of change and decay in all around. What, indeed, of any child who was born into a world so unreliable and hostile that he or she could never build up any basic trust in it or in his or her own worth?

I was blessed with a happy and secure start to life which has enabled me, just about, to cope with disappointment and suffering. What of the emotionally starved and crippled, the chronically depressed and mentally unstable? Unlike some of my colleagues, I have not had a great deal of experience in trying to bring some measure of self-worth to these suffering people, though inevitably I have come across many in my life as a priest and social worker. When I was beginning to train for the latter I spent a morning with a forensic psychiatrist. He interviewed a boy of fourteen who had been unspeakably cruel to younger children. He talked about his childhood in which he was beaten and left alone by his parents. After the session I asked the psychiatrist what would happen to the boy. He said he would go to a detention centre and that he was a hopeless case; he would end up in Broadmoor, an incurable psychopath. I couldn't then and cannot now accept that nothing can be done to help young people of this kind. In my experience there is nearly always someone who was kind, someone who gave the child an idea of what love is, something to work on. If there wasn't, then I believe it is possible to begin from scratch and help a person learn to love by being loved. If priests or social workers, whatever their past failures, stop believing that change is possible then their work becomes impossible. If Christian talk of incarnation means anything at all it surely means that God thinks it worth while to identify with the human race and suffer with us. Many people tell me that their life has been changed for the better because of a kind word at the right time, and many have told me it was I who gave it, though nearly always I have forgotten the incident and certainly not understood its significance.

What I do find very difficult is to feel of any use to people who are deeply depressed. I have sat for hours with them, and everything I have suggested was met with silence or a negative answer. I would give up talking, except to describe how many others have felt when depressed, and would perhaps get nods of agreement. I would leave the interview feeling heavy, sad and useless. When the depressed person recovered I would perhaps say how useless, and invariably receive the reply that my mere presence was a help. 'You came, and continued to come.' Many doctors and priests fear the heart-sinkers and fail to discern the value of visiting even when they think they can do 'nothing' for them. Their coming and giving reassurance will already be a help. 'Dr Finlay came and did nothing but I felt much better for it' is not a figment of the imagination.

Grief will come to us all. The sensitive friend or therapist can help us come to terms with bereavement, which in the end means that we accept the reality that a loved one has gone for ever and we let them go. This is a terribly difficult work to be got through, especially as the sufferer is already debilitated by the loss. It may not be hurried either, and is more likely to take two or three years than six or seven months. After all, it takes many years of growth and development for someone to become a rounded, adult person, more or less complete within him- or herself. Then he or she enters a close relationship with another person, perhaps in marriage, perhaps in a close business partnership or profound friendship. As the relationship moulds both persons they begin to shape themselves to accommodate the other. If the relationship is reasonably successful, each partner will learn to be resilient where the other is rigid, able to receive where the other needs to give, to be strong where the other is weak, to complement each other at various levels. As the union becomes more complex this complementarity will involve a dovetailing into each other on emotional as well as sexual levels, and on the spiritual and intellectual, physical and practical levels as well. It will include job sharing and supporting each other's interests and hobbies. Eventually each partner will have ceased being an autonomous person and will have become half of a whole, interlocking with the other into a mutual enfolding which is expressed and deepened in the sexual embrace. When one partner goes away for good it leaves the other still in this incomplete shape because he or she had become moulded to accommodate and fit into the partner. The bereaved one is no longer complete but still feels half of a whole even though the other half is not there. The process of growing into a new, independent, complete rounded person will be a long and painful one. If in the early stages of loss the bereaved partner tries to enter into a new relationship it will present all sorts of problems because the person will for a time be still adapted to a previous shape of union which had its individual, mutual contours formed over the years. There are homely expressions that bring this out – 'new wine will burst old wineskins', 'one cannot wear another's shoes', and ' 'tis best to be off with the old love before being on with the new'.

A child will at first cling to its mother and cannot bear separation for more than brief intervals without suffering anxiety. Gradually it will learn to internalize its mother, to carry her love and regard within itself so that the child can be physically separated from her without stress because she is in some sense within it and can never be lost. The same process will often facilitate and characterize the work of grieving. The bereft 'half' person will incorporate into his or her personality those precious elements of the other that meant so much in the relationship. In that way he or she can never again be completely separated from the loved one. I saw an example of this in my father who hitherto had rarely written to his children or grandchildren. My mother had always remembered Christmas and birthdays but after she died my father spontaneously carried on the generous office and to this day, many years later, sends cards and presents without fail to his numerous extended family. I also know many widows who previously left the gardening or greenhouse to their husband and now take on both after their husband's death. In some close unions one partner rather overshadows the other, and the one who is left has a time to blossom on his or her own. Bereavement is not all loss. My own bereavement has allowed me to develop a close relationship with my children that may not have been at all so easily realized in marriage.

The disciples, of course, went through this kind of thing on a grand scale. According to John's Gospel, Jesus told them: 'It is for your own good that I am going because unless I go, the Advocate will not come to you; but if I do go I will send him to you' (John 16:7). He could therefore say, in another passage, 'I shall not leave you orphans: I shall come to you' (John 14:18).

There simply are times in life when we have to let go of what we think is important, even essential, in order to grow. Such are also times of crisis, and a parent does well to help a son or daughter going off to college or university to cope with the transition. In the same way we need particularly to nurture the bereaved and gradually help them to find themselves again as independent persons capable of forming new relationships and of opening new areas of life and interest with some enthusiasm. It is a dangerous time because despair can so easily undermine any attempt if it is made too soon. Under strain we regress, take to our bed, need indulging and being taken care of. I wonder whether some teenagers become aggressive and difficult with their previously loved and admired parents and siblings because parting from them is so demanding a change that they cannot make it unless to some extent they rubbish those they are to leave in order to make leaving more bearable. Often, like the colonial abroad, they will take aspects of their loved family with them and be more like their parent than they ever could dare to be at home.

We have to lose life in order to find it. If nothing else in the New Testament is truly the very saying as Jesus spoke it, I believe this one is. It is so *him*. Grieving is a gift of life, the cost of loving, the last token we can give to the beloved. Although grieving people are sometimes stigmatized as being self-indulgent, they are in fact giving unconditional love to the one who has left – they can gain nothing from their tears, no gratitude or recognition from the beloved for whom they are shed. It is pure unselfish generous love, their grief, and deserves respect. But, as with the disciples pictured in the Gospel gazing up to heaven at the ascending Christ, some angel needs sooner or later to come to us and kindly say, 'Why look up? – he has gone – you go back to Galilee and get on with the work he left you to do.'

Many of my friends have told me that since leaving the priesthood I have become more open and approachable. What I can offer is offered of my freedom and not because of my office. I do not regret for a moment all that being a priest enabled me to experience and so in some way to use still for others. And since divorce, with the help of the counsellor and much more of the beloved friend who has sustained me through the last years with her love and belief in my worth, I know I have become far more of a man, more responsible, more aware, more able to give. I am confident that death itself, although I want to postpone it because there is much I still want to try and do for others and for myself in this life, will bring, in some mysterious yet continuous and dimly apprehended way, anything of good in my life that I have begun in this womb of a world. We cling to one another and dread being alone, yet know that we were born alone and will die alone, and both can bring new, undreamt of wonderful possibilities of loving and giving most freely and willingly. Jesus the man died, but his spirit is now free to be everywhere, to the extent we let him be. He works through us who, like Jesus the archetype, are sons and daughters of God whose life is one of giving.

5

WRESTLING WITH VOCATION

The other day I asked Joe, my 11-year-old son, 'Why are we on earth?' He answered at once, 'We don't need to know, it's mysteries that keep us going.' Having apparently made two major mistakes in the past by assuming I was called to the priesthood in the first place and marriage in the second, I find the business of rediscovering my vocation now is one of those mysteries.

In church terms both sacraments were validly celebrated and I lived them out as far as I was able, and both ways of life collapsed. Can I ever again trust that I have a 'vocation'? Like others in my position and with similar religious antecedents, I am sometimes haunted by the two biblical texts relating to these states of life. The first is 'Thou art a priest forever', and the second 'What God has joined together, let no man put asunder'. If taken at face value, such commands seem to me to reflect an essentialist view of God and the world. They begin by defining what something intrinsically is, its essence, and then go on to draw inferences – priesthood *is* a cultic power, a grace conferred, a status given that cannot be lost even if one is dispensed from any obligation to exercise it. Marriage *is* a binding, lasting, unbreakable contract that binds until the death of one partner.

On the other hand, if I look at these callings in an existential light I shall be inclined to define priesthood by the abiding, everlasting need of the Christian community to celebrate its priestly identity through the ministry of an ordained representative in here and now circumstances that are ever changing. And it is at least possible to see marriage not in terms of contract but of relationship. If this relationship effectively breaks down, or if one party unilaterally walks out of it for good, the couple are *ipso facto* no longer in a marriage. There is no longer any marriage.

I shall return to these specific examples of vocational life later in the chapter. Before doing so, I would prefer to look at vocation in a wider context altogether. As a Catholic brought up in the Judaeo-Christian stream of religious tradition I shall consider vocation only from this standpoint. In doing so I do not wish in any way to undervalue any other tradition, or the holiness and integrity which characterize so many individuals in their search for discerning the will of God for them. It's just that I don't know enough about these traditions to feel qualified to comment on them.

For Christians, then, the call of God may be seen to be exemplified in the life of Abraham, of Moses and, *par excellence*, of Jesus himself. Abraham was called away 'into a land I *will* show you' and he lived and died by faith, in expectation, not knowing where his journey would take him but repeatedly depending upon God to show him. If ever a man travelled hopefully, he did. Moses was called to lead his people into freedom after greater hardships, yet he himself saw the promised land only from afar. Neither of them could see how God's promise would be fulfilled, but lived in the faith that it would be. Jesus too learnt obedience through suffering, alone and in silent tears. His death was apparent failure, as he cried out to ask why his Father had abandoned him. The last chapter of the letter to the Hebrews calls on us to follow these leaders in the faith: 'Remember your leaders, who preached the word of God to you, and as you reflect on the outcome of their lives, imitate their faith.' The whole chapter reads like a commentary on the words of Micah: 'This is what the Lord asks of you: to act justly, to love tenderly and to walk humbly with your God' (6:8). This waiting on God is surely the primary vocation for a Christian and indeed for every seeker in every religion.

Secondary to this universal call is vocation in the special and traditional Christian sense of God's call to a particular way of life which will put us at his disposal for the good of the Church as a whole. Each person has to discern how he is being called and to what service. The Christian communities in the early centuries were aware that they had a right to a minister or ministers for the celebration of the eucharist. This apostolic right comes from the invitation of Jesus himself: 'Do this in memory of me'. It has priority over the criteria for admission to the ministry which the

Church may impose on its ministers. Schillebeeckx (*Ministry: A Case for Change*) writes that ministry in the Church is not 'a status or state but a service, a function within the community of God and therefore a gift of the Holy Spirit'. He quotes the Council of Chalcedon (AD 451): 'Only someone who has been called by a particular community and its leaders to be its pastor and leader authentically receives *ordinatio*.' The same Council states that an 'absolute' *ordinatio*, by which is meant ordination independent of a community, is null and void. Schillebeeckx also quotes what St Cyprian wrote two centuries earlier: 'No bishop is to be imposed on the people whom they do not want.' After Chalcedon, a minister who ceased to be president over a community *ipso facto* returned to being a layman. This emphasis on the call to ministry for the building up of the local community through the eucharist was commonly seen as its *raison d'être*. However, the right to the eucharist for the community was paramount and apparently preceded even the call and appointment of an ordained minister, according to Tertullian: 'When no college of ministers has been appointed, you the laity must celebrate the eucharist and baptize.' What a long way we have moved from these early directives!

It was recognized from the earliest days that one chosen to be a minister should be fit for such a service. The letter to Timothy refers to a received tradition on the matter:

> Here is a saying that you can rely on: to want to be a presiding elder is to want to do a noble work. That is why the president must have an impeccable character. He must not be married more than once, and he must be temperate, discreet and courteous, hospitable and a good teacher; not a heavy drinker, nor hot tempered, but kind and peaceable. He must not be a lover of money. He must be a man who manages his own family well and brings his children up to obey him and be well-behaved; how can any man who does not understand how to manage his own family have responsibility for the Church of God? (1 Timothy 3:1–5, JB)

These expectations are only specific qualities most appropriate to the leader of the community in which every member is called to holiness and perfection. The Church as a whole is called to be a communion of saints, a sign of Christ's continuing presence in the world, just as Christ is the sign of God's.

If all are called to be holy, then the huge moral weight imposed on the ordained ministers of the Church over the centuries will be seen in context. Hitherto, the priest has often been almost identified with the Church itself, as in the expression 'he's gone into the Church' meaning 'he's going to be ordained'. He has been seen, still is very often, as over and above the Church in a sort of senior rank. If indeed he is set apart, pre-eminently reflecting in his life and work what the call to perfection means, he is only one among many who are called in their own walk of life to love tenderly and walk humbly with their God.

This brings me to an area of theology that has bothered me for years. There has been an expectation within the Catholic Church for at least the last seven centuries, culminating in the reforms of the Council of Trent (1545–1563), that the clergy should be outstanding in holiness of life and be celibate as well. They should live as near a monastic life as possible while still being at large in the world, unprotected and unsupported by community life within a monastery. Until very recently, the priest was expected seven times a day to recite the divine office which monks sing collectively in the abbey church – matins and lauds, prime, terce, sext, none, vespers and compline, corresponding to prayer in the very early hours, prayer on rising, prayer at 9, 12 and 3 o'clock respectively, prayer in the evening and again before bed. It was a grave obligation under pain of sin. He was also expected to celebrate mass every day, whether anybody came or not. He was supposed to wear clerical dress at all times, which on the European continent meant clerical collar and cassock and even clerical hat, well into the present century. He was a man set apart and was meant to look like it. The fact that in an increasingly secular and industrialized society he would look as out of place as would a judge in court wig and robes walking down the high street on his own, a relic of the Middle Ages mingling in the supermarket of life, apparently counted for nothing.

Hand in hand with this obligation to live as a man apart, 'in the world but not of it', there was a pervasive theological principle which insisted that, independently of the worthiness of the priest, sacraments correctly administered were always valid. Everything depended upon the correctness of the ritual and the right intention of the priest. Pushed to its extreme, this would mean that a half-drunken priest who had spend the night with his lover and stolen from parish funds to give her money, could nonetheless quite validly say mass or hear confessions in the morning. The holiness of the action was nothing to do with the holiness of the minister though, on the other hand, the lay recipient of the sacrament *had* to be in the right dispositions or it would be ineffective, for him or her. Various would-be reformers during the Middle Ages protested against making sacraments into 'things' in this way, and favoured the opposite principle that emphasizes the need for worthiness in both priest and recipient for a sacrament to be efficacious. The former view, however, prevailed, one hopes in order to underline the primacy of God's grace rather than human worthiness in sacramental matters. Perhaps it also prevailed for the less worthy reason that it gave enormous spiritual power and control to the clergy. Those were the days when popes could lay an interdict upon a country, perhaps for political reasons, which effectively barred the laity from receiving the sacraments altogether. It also gave rise to widespread abuse, as evidenced by the thousands of 'massing priests' before the Reformation, whose sole function was to say masses in chantry chapels for the souls of dead benefactors. It was their income, but often enough they lived in a way that was alien to the gospel and almost nothing to do with a local community except in the most tenuous sense.

My generation of priests, like so many before us, was thus brought up in a religious culture which both imposed rigid high ideals on the priest but at the same time gave him sacramental powers that were independent of whether he lived those ideals or not. Many colleagues certainly lived them out with utter single-mindedness and dedication. Many others were lazy functionaries who did a minimum, lived in a privileged way with a comfortable house and housekeeper (in the sixties!), three cooked meals a day and so on, and had little apparent sense of the Church as community or themselves as its servants.

What I came to detest was not the priestly role and office, let alone the vocation to dedicated service, but the clericalization of the men who exercised that office. To concentrate power, authority, control over people and money, over the building of churches and schools, over the appointment of teachers and admission of pupils, over the furnishing and decoration of all church buildings, all in the hands of one parish priest answerable in those days to nobody except the bishop, was to ask of these priests that they be both powerful and humble at the same time. Until the 1960s there were no parish councils, no avenues for constructive criticism to reach the clergy, no structured partnership between priest and people except where through the grace and favour of an enlightened priest such possibilities were opened up by him, perhaps to be closed again by his successor. The shape of the liturgy expressed the clericalism of the priesthood: with his back to the people the priest would say mass in Latin with barely any reference to the people at all. They were expected to pay up and shut up. In 1959 I remember being called in to the parish church for the Good Friday liturgy. The old priest who was celebrating asked me to provide a commentary from the pulpit and to read the account of the passion in English while he got on with the liturgy in Latin. This was forward looking at the time and I was duly delighted. But to my dismay he gabbled so fast through the Latin of the Gospel that I was only half way through when he had finished. Instead of waiting for me to end, he simply went on with the mass and I had to give up. Most of the people who had crowded into the church didn't have a missal in English and certainly knew no Latin, so the prayers and readings of most of the service were totally inaccessible to them. But to the clerical mind it mattered not at all: the liturgy had been performed, the words and actions were correct, never mind what effect they had on the people present.

It seemed to me then and seems to me now, when much has changed for the better, that there are two views of priesthood within the Catholic Church, which I may perhaps call the high and the low. The high view is that ordination confers a special dignity upon a man and essentially changes his spiritual status, just as baptism does. A baptized person remains a member of the Church whatever he or she does, as a member of a family remains a son or daughter whether he or she loses communication with them or stays close. A priest is always a priest, even if he resigns. In his office, the priest is 'another Christ' and acts 'in the person of Christ'. The bishop is a direct successor of the apostles in an unbroken line, and priests are his assistants in communion with him and sharing his apostolic power. One can be a priest without a parish or community to look after, as are many monks, and officials in the Vatican and elsewhere. Ordination, the call to exercise spiritual power, is conferred by the laying on of hands by a bishop. It is defined by cult. This high view will tend, though not necessarily so, to clericalism.

The low view tends to see ministry not as a status conferred but as a service to be given. The character, holiness and human qualities of the priest will be of great importance if he is to be an effective leader and builder of the community. Solidarity with the poor and insignificant is an essential mark of the apostolicity of his work. The recognition of and sending by the Church is the primary meaning of ordination, and priesthood is defined more by the service given to the community than by the cultic clerical state.

I am talking of two views that are not necessarily in contradiction with each other, and am aware that some priests combine both in their office and personal gifts. I was reflecting on this the other month when I read an amusing article in *The Times* of 1 January 1993. It was called 'Britain's secret civil war', written by Matthew d'Ancona. He argued that we are all romantic Cavaliers or Puritan Roundheads at heart:

> The cavalier, as everyone knows, is extravagant, indulgent, flamboyant, indiscreet, spontaneous, optimistic and libidinous; the roundhead is disciplined, pessimistic, frugal, discreet, sober and sexually restrained . . .
>
> In the 17th century, the two sides fought in uniform, but now the social observer has to know the tell tale signs to distinguish the roundhead on the Clapham omnibus from the cavalier in the chauffeur-driven car. Cavaliers continue to like their religion high rather than low, for example, though they are wary of the 'smells and bells' lobby. Though they rarely, if ever, set foot in a church, cavaliers will happily engage in saloon-bar banter to defend the old-fashioned liturgy. Most of them oppose female ordination and are definitely suspicious of Archbishop Carey, an unreconstructed roundhead.

My human sympathies are more like the Cavalier than the Roundhead, yet in my opinion the low view of the priesthood (not very Cavalier) is more in keeping with the spirit of the gospel than the high. Just as it was easy for a friend of mine recently to wander again round St Peter's in Rome and wonder what on earth any of this glory had to do with the gospel, so it was until recently quite normal to attend an episcopal high mass and be forgiven for thinking it did not much look like a Last Supper where, far from wearing gorgeous vestments, the chief celebrant put a towel round his waist and washed his disciples' feet.

These high and low views coexist in curious ways at the present time. I recently went to a lovely abbey church for Sunday mass and to my pleasure a monk was to be ordained deacon during it. The clergy – bishops, abbots, secular priests, monks – and the choir were robed in the splendid sanctuary and the whole service could have taken place very amply even if there had been no lay people in the far off nave at all. The lights, the decoration, the altar, the action, the singing for the main part – all took place in the sanctuary. This was benign clericalism, an initiation into a clerical order. The bishop was well aware that deacons are ordained to be of service to the people of God, and his sermon was to the point and in no way condescending. He stressed the calling to service many times. Yet the nature of our liturgy that day made it look all the other way round. The people who sat in the best seats at the 'top table' were the 'servants' and they ate and drank the spiritual food and drink first. Then they brought some down the nave to the people. I did not feel they were in any remote way 'at our service'. If they were, priests and people would have all intermingled throughout and the priests would have made sure they served the people before having their own meal afterwards. Or all would have eaten and drunk in no particular order of precedence at all.

The high, sometimes clerical, view of priesthood tends to remove clergy from close mingling with people in general and is more at ease with the state of celibacy which has been a prerequisite of ordination for so long. It can and does produce priests of high calibre and integrity, many of whom are kind and unpretentious men. It is fearful of the ordination of women and I think it likely to be more compatible with a reading of the New Testament that does not give too much weight to modern biblical criticism and analysis. Its extreme proponents probably take it for granted that at the Last Supper Jesus was ordaining the twelve (male) apostles when he told them, 'Do this in memory of me.' Some of them have told me they still see me as a priest but doing a different kind of ministry because married. Part of me feels the same.

The low view tends, I think, to bring priest and people closer and to minimize the difference between them. Ideally the community would choose their candidate from among their number and put him or her forward as their choice for the ministry. They would also want the local communities together to elect their own bishop, as they used to centuries ago. The low view is not threatened so much by liberal textual criticism of the New Testament, and would prefer to think of 'orders' as being a way the followers of Christ after the resurrection decided for themselves to ensure the handing on of the message and way of life Jesus had taught. They would see the ministry as having changed its form in various ways, especially in the early centuries, and would not be disturbed by a variety of priestly ministries: both men and women, married and celibate, monastic and diocesan, those working already for other paid employment and those who are full-time ministers and dependent on the Church for their living.

My view, though inevitably mixed, inclines to the low. I never felt particularly 'priestly' even in my most dedicated days, and although I received many generous tributes for the work I did, I have often been told since that various people thought my heart wasn't really in it. I certainly never thanked God that I was a priest, any more than I now thank him that I am a social worker. What I do thank him for is the joy of trying to be of some use to people, the joy of being human, the gift of life itself and of course the gift of faith. In the past, people came to me with personal problems and expected both good counsel and a sense of spiritual direction and support. Now they come, sometimes for the same but more often for help on the human and psychological level. In many ways the two 'ministries' are similar: both are in some way to do with the *anawim*, the poor, the unhappy, the lost, the lame and the deaf and the blind. Both are in some ways work for the kingdom. I still have the particular vocation I had before – to be a 'people person', there for others, accessible and supportive when invited to be so. I do wonder whether in a curious way the being there for others (which I love) also means that God wants me to live alone (which I don't love).

I will turn now to the vocational state of marriage, in the sense that it is a single-minded devotion to a way of life and helps to build up the Christian community. I said above that in the early Church ordination meant a commitment to serve the community. If a priest left the community for other work, he ceased to be a priest. In the same way, I believe that as long as two people are in a relationship that is feasible and mutually enriching, they are in a marriage (whether in the strict sense or not) and should honour the commitment. What I cannot see is why a partner should remain in a married relationship which is dead with no hope of revival. Much psychological harm is done to priests who stay on out of fear or a sense of duty, and they cease to be life-giving for others, being half dead themselves. The same is true of loveless marriages: what is the good of continuing in them? Is a marriage a state of life to be contractually entered into and never left, whatever the circumstances? Must we take literally the words 'What God has joined together, let not man put asunder'? Was not the Bishop of Repton right when in 1980 he suggested 'Let no man hold together what God has graciously allowed to fall apart'?

The traditional requirements for a marriage to be a fully Christian one are that it should be freely entered into by a baptized couple, that it is validly celebrated and consummated afterwards. If any of these elements is missing, the marriage can be declared invalid or null. These conditions are recent in the history of the Church. The Church has only required marriage to be witnessed by a priest since the thirteenth century, and it was not defined as a sacrament until the sixteenth. It was the freely made *contract* that was regarded as the 'stuff' of the sacrament, and its indissoluble nature rested upon the marriage being a faithful reflection of the love of Christ for his Church. This insistence upon its indissolubility is peculiar to the western Church; the tradition in the Orthodox Church is to allow remarriage in certain circumstances.

The Second Vatican Council, in its decree on *The Church in the Modern World* (para 47–52), and even the encyclical *Humanae Vitae* in 1968 have a different approach that is less insistent upon the nature of an unbreakable contract and more in line with contemporary insights. They affirm that the life-giving interpersonal *relationship* between the couple is the 'stuff' of the marriage, rather then the *contract*. This relationship indeed implies permanent and exclusive love and is described as a covenant of interpersonal love which is faithful and life-giving. Giving life is a lifelong process, hence the need for permanence. The Synod of Bishops in 1980 speaks of the giving of life to the children of the marriage and states that their education goes on until the children are 'brought fully alive'. Marriage is not, therefore, so much an institution which people enter into as an interpersonal reality which the couple bring about. Indissolubility is being seen by many in the Church, if not by the officials of the Church, as a task to be undertaken by the couple and is consequent upon the unconditional, life-giving love necessary to sustain such a relationship.

The actual fact is that Christian marriages in the West break down just as much as any others. In his *Marital Breakdown*, Dr Jack Dominian gives a table of features that all breakdowns have in common: one or both of the partners is emotionally unstable, immature and critical of other people, dominating, isolated, lacking self-confidence and appearing to be emotionally self-sufficient. He writes:

> Marital failure is ultimately associated with the presence of one or both partners who have only partially or incompletely negotiated the various phases (i.e. of emotional independence of parents, trust, self-acceptance, ability to receive and donate of self to the other and an absence of excessive anxiety and aggression) and the spouse is chosen as a means to complete growth which should have been completed prior to marriage, or to supply vital personal needs missing during the period of (childhood) development.

A child's parenting must be good enough for the child to reach wholeness. The child must achieve basic trust, confidence and self-value if it is to be truly independent as an adult. In marriage, a couple must be able to establish a similar level of basic trust if they are to experience themselves as truly a couple, two in one flesh. The union needed and sought will be guaranteed not by the external sanction against divorce, not by mere physical and contractual union, but by a profound personal rapport at the important levels – intellectual, spiritual and emotional as well as physical.

Dominian goes on to write that there are typical and necessary stages through which a marriage will pass, but that the real needs of a partner will not emerge until the previous stage is completed. So a girl may marry a father-substitute either because she is immature and wished to repeat a good father–daughter relationship, or because she looks for the good father–daughter relationship she never really experienced in childhood. The husband may collude and the transaction will be that of adult to child, or parent to child. But when her real adult needs emerge and she seeks to be her mature self there will be a profound and traumatic change in the relationship. It may well be that neither party will have the knowledge, wisdom and experience, let alone the trust and patience or other resources to understand what is happening to them or to negotiate the crisis.

In a remarkable book *Divorce and Second Marriage*, Kevin Kelly, a highly respected moral theologian, wrote in 1982 that marital breakdown may well be unavoidable and without wilful sin in either party, because the ability to give and receive love is absent. There isn't sufficient emotional maturity for an adult love relationship:

> Marriage and marital love consist in clearly identifiable components which must operate at a minimum level and some of them are outside the control of the couple . . . a marriage may die . . . because the couple did not know how to love each other.

In traditional language this may be called emotional impotence, which is really equivalent to non-consummation of the marriage except in a purely physical sense.

I prefer the wisdom of these two experienced and profoundly human writers to routine tired pronouncements from the Vatican or truisms from Church officials when they simply repeat old formulae and burden lay people with loads they do not carry themselves. I should perhaps add that I have a corresponding admiration for couples who, supported by the traditional teaching, and refusing to contemplate the possibility of separation, slog on and do in fact reach a whole relationship with their partner. They may have once thought that this was impossible owing to some block or immaturity that was rendering the relationship non-viable, but they came through with the help of good counselling and much courage. That is the way I would have tried myself had I been given the option. But if one party feels compelled to leave what to him or her has become an intolerable living death, I do not think anything but understanding and support are appropriate. The difficulty is for the Church to give equal support to those who try to battle through without appearing to reject those who have tried and failed.

It was difficult for me to recover a sense of direction when my marriage failed. In an earlier chapter I described how I preserved what I could by remaining on as good terms as possible with my wife who had left, by being as available as possible to the children and by staying in the same lane we had lived in. All three ways have borne good fruit. It is much more difficult to know what is the next step to take in this funny old journey through life. Sometimes I have felt that God was leading me on, in the sense of having me on. I have just about weathered the years of searing loneliness and come to terms with being by myself during the week. I have been greatly helped by my beloved woman friend but cannot be with her in the immediate future. What does God want of me now? How am I to know? It habitually seems to me that in some ways I am still living a vocational life, in that the work of trying to be more aware of God, of my neighbour and of myself goes on. I think all three (are they divisible?) have been mysteriously deepened by the very trauma I would have avoided if I could. A nun friend wrote to me: 'You have emerged from the trauma of your marriage with a courage and a humbleness which was far less evident before, and whatever else has contributed to these the most important is the quality and depth of your simple, classical spirituality and relationship with God as Father.'

I think that sometimes we don't know which way we should go. We only know which way not to go. But even the next step can be a difficult one to take. I know that what friends reflect to me is of very great importance in telling me whether I am still on the road at all, let alone the right one. I believe that if I continue to pray, watching and waiting and silent, God will show the way. Books, too, are a help. Anthony Storr's *Solitude* spells out cogently how much there is to be said for and positively gained by embracing a solitary life. St Bernard of Clairvaux said it also, less helpfully, centuries ago: '*O beata solitudo! O sola beatitudo!*' But then, he was a saint.

So, I travel hopefully, not struggling any more against the solitude I so dreaded. I think I may at last have come to a sort of acceptance, provided I don't examine it too closely, that at least for the time being I am alone and that it is in many ways, like everything God has made, very good. It has at the very least made me more sensitive to the pain of loss and confusion felt by so many people, and has forced me to be more and more aware of my inner being. Silence in this part of Suffolk is silence indeed, especially at night, but it is no longer an empty silence. Sometimes it feels like a supreme gift I could no longer do without. So often when friends come into the cottage their first exclamation is 'Oh, how peaceful and welcoming!' If that peacefulness is really within my deepest self, and the ability to make others welcome continues to be one of the chief joys of my life, then perhaps I don't have to look further for a vocation to make itself clear.

6

PRIESTHOOD
AND SOCIAL WORK

Years ago someone said to me, 'Your work is with people.' In this chapter I should like to say something about the nature of such work within the settings of the priesthood and of social services. May I begin with an example from each.

In the early sixties, when everyone wore hats and the clergy wore black, when Catholics went regularly to confession and the Second Vatican Council had not yet unsettled traditional ways of thinking, a young woman from another parish came to talk to me after mass. She was struggling with guilt, failure and anger. Her marriage had been loveless, and she finally left her unfaithful husband. She brought up her four children unaided, in a draughty town house with all the miseries attendant upon genteel poverty and, in those days, the opprobrium of divorce. She found relief in going to confession and talking over her feelings, because it made her feel accepted and forgiven. She loved going to mass and was active in her own parish, but was tempted to turn her back on the Church and marry again. Somehow she couldn't, because she felt her religion was her one strength and stay.

In those days I had no doubts about my own similar conviction that I too should persevere, despite the longing to find comfort in a normal relationship with a woman. I was still absolutely celibate, and she often said that if I could cope with that then so could she. I saw her regularly through the years until her children married, and then lost touch for many years.

By the time we met again she was grey and lined but still beautiful and still alone. She had found peace with herself, her religion and with her persona as a social worker. By then I had not only left the priesthood but my own marriage had failed. She said it didn't really matter. I could still go on trying to help others to find peace and fulfilment: 'Your heart has been broken and at last you understand.'

Ten years after that meeting I am writing this chapter and mourning the death of an aged client. He first came to my attention when neighbours expressed concern because they had not seen him or his wife leave the house for weeks. I found the curtains shut, and the door unanswered. Eventually I made contact by putting messages through the letter box. He wrote back that they were 'all right thank you'. Peering through, I could dimly see his wife on the sofa. Friends did their shopping for them so I knew they had some contact with the outside world. Four years later he summoned help when his wife had a stroke and was admitted to hospital. She was covered with burns and abrasions and could not speak. I gained entry to the house and over the next three years he was seen regularly by the nurse, the psychiatrist, the GP, the home carer and myself. He would only let the nurse tend his painful leg, the home carer do his shopping. He would talk rationally for a while and then slip into a sort of time warp and describe the war in Germany as if in the present. His paranoia was so strong that at times he imagined I was the military police. The enemy were trying to lay siege to the house so he barricaded it and patrolled it all night, setting booby traps for any intruder. He never went to bed and often hardly ate enough to survive. But he did, and we felt we should help him to stay at home as long as possible. At other times he thought I was a court official, so he talked of his proud war record and showed me tributes from past employers as if to substantiate his good character and innocence. He would let me bring him electric fires and cigarettes, but then turn suspicious and accuse me of breaking in and stealing his savings certificates, of heading the Diss mafia and sending spies dressed up as nurses. The fires would be pulled to pieces, the electrics failed, the gas oven blew up. He would not leave the house except when friends took him to see his wife in hospital or I took him to the bank. He would not go into care and would I please bring his wife back to him? On a good day he would talk with complete command of his reason and memory, and it was then that his infinitely sad comments that he had lost everything would move me profoundly. When I left he would doff his military hat and bow politely. At last he too was admitted to hospital, after which we found a place for him in one of our local authority Homes. Within four riotous days in which he stood drinks and was courtesy personified to everyone, he developed an infection, had a massive stroke and died. The night he was dying, the manager of the Home, a good friend of mine, as perceptive as he is tenderhearted, rang me at home. 'Tell him he is forgiven,' I asked. Later he told me that he had sat with Bill as he was dying. Bill said he hated some people. The manager said: 'You don't want to go to sleep hating anybody do you?' 'No sir, you're right, I don't.' He died peacefully soon after. When a colleague and I went through the house to safeguard any valuables we found twelve dustbin bags full of rubbish in a back bedroom. He had thrown everything away including his cheque book, savings certificates, the photograph of his wife, his clothes. The house was almost empty except for his war medals laid out on the desk. I have known few people travel so lightly into the next life, or whose leaving this one has so moved me.

These are only two instances of the kind of work familiar to priests and social workers, and indeed everyone in the caring professions, but they exemplify two features I have found are constants in my work. One is that I think parishioners and clients would be surprised to know how deeply they have touched my inner self, how I have loved them, learnt from them, felt humbled and exhilarated by them. The other is that I find it as impossible to distinguish many aspects of priestly and social work from each other as I do to distinguish between the spiritual and human qualities of people. I do not mean to reduce priestly work to the simply human, nor would I dream of suggesting to agnostic colleagues that their humanitarian work often typifies for me the good news of the kingdom. But Christianity is incarnational through and through, and I do not think the social work I now do is radically different from the priestly work I used to do. As my younger brother, Bryan, wrote in a letter:

> You seem to me to be far more practical, understanding and tolerant than you were twenty years ago, but you may have become all these things within the priesthood. You weren't necessarily going to follow the general pattern, but I think you would have been likely to. You are thriving on being free of the restrictions you used to be under, and yet I can easily

see you as a priest again under a modified régime . . . I think you do as a layman work which any genuinely Christian priest would spend a lot of his time doing anyway, so, to a certain extent, you are still what you were ordained to be.

Some months ago I gave a talk in Norwich. One of those attending asked if she could come to me for counselling. The talk had been similar to those I give to social-work students on the subject of loss and bereavement, except that, as it was a religious group, I emphasized the way in which God may use our human skill to do his healing work. The sessions I had with this person were likewise a mixture of straight counselling and of purely spiritual direction. One flowed from and into the other all the time.

It seems to me somewhat sad that the Church has in the past so spiritualized much of its message that the world has no time for it in helping with humankind's more earthly needs and dilemmas. And yet in many ways it has attended to both, as exemplified by the massive contribution of nuns and priests in the active and contemplative orders – teaching, nursing, giving hospitality and counsel and so on. I knew too, as a priest, that the parishioners who spent most time in prayer were the very ones I could ask to do practical work like visiting the sick, helping with overseas aid, relieving poverty. Human life will not allow itself to be divided into the spiritual and the material, the holy and the whole, the world to come and the world here and now. The two interpenetrate all the time, even if we sometimes get the emphasis wrong. So I would like now to look at some of the similarities and contrasts I have found in being a priest and in being a social worker, although I am hesitant about drawing too sharp a distinction between them.

In both professional ways of life, the priest and social worker are instrumental in bringing resources to people. In one case the resources are spiritual: the grace of God is conveyed through the sacraments and brings life, nourishment, healing and reconcili-ation. In the other they are more material: people are taken into care and placed in Homes, help is brought to them in their homes, problems are sorted out by the use of personal and psychological skills. But what seems to matter most in both cases is the manner in which the resources are mediated. If I go to mass and the priest smiles, looks at us as he speaks, creates an atmosphere of mutual trust and warmth, I come away feeling restored. If he is perfunctory and detached, performing the liturgy in a formalized, impersonal way, avoiding human contact and engagement with the people, I come away feeling much less rich. The personality and style of the priest make a great difference. If the priest himself looks and sounds like good news, then whatever the liturgy or sermon are like I will feel better for it. If he is not good news then all the correct ritual will leave me cold. In the same way, a social worker will, for example, admit a frail old woman into a Home. She will be safe and warm and well looked after in more or less agreeable surroundings. How she feels about it will depend very largely on the social worker's ability to make her feel understood, valued and cared for. If the worker helps the person to express sadness because of having to give up independence, home, old associations, possessions; if he shows that he understands how traumatic such a change is and talks about it, then the client will view the whole business with more comfort and confidence than if it is handled in an impersonal, official, unfeeling sort of way.

It does dismay me when more importance is attached to the look of things than to the feel of things. A priest may build a church that is modern, bright, comfortable, liturgically correct and well appointed, but if he himself lacks love it will feel empty and cold. The same applies to Homes for elderly people; much more depends upon the kindness of the person in charge than on the décor of the building. I have seen plenty of children thriving in a leaky Victorian school building with kind, human teachers. I know old people in equally old-fashioned Homes where there is a good atmosphere, and they are happy.

One of the troubles, I think, is that it is far easier for a bishop to ensure that external standards are maintained than it is for him to enthuse and inspire the clergy. If a priest, or any other leader in the Church, feels appreciated and trusted and supported by those above, he or she will tend to communicate confidently the same sort of care to those receiving their ministrations. If he or she feels isolated, suspect, depressed by the latest pronouncements of the pope or curia then this is bound to show in the way his or her pastoral work is done.

The social worker too will feel and behave differently depending on how he or she is treated by senior managers. It is easier for a bureaucratic management to issue endless rules of procedure from the safety of County Hall than it is for them to mix among field workers, show that they understand what the worker is trying to do and what the difficulties are, and provide the encouragement and resources which will inspire the worker to go on doing a difficult task.

Middle managers are even more important to the field worker. I have indicated in previous chapters how much I was affected by the parish priests I was under. In social work, if the team manager values and trusts the worker then the latter feels that what he or she does is not only valuable to the client but is also approved of by management. This matters greatly. It affects the worker's ability to go on giving to and helping the clients. Happily, this is so in my own case. But if the worker feels his or her work is not valued, if no supervision is offered and no real support given, he or she may go on doing it for sheer love of the clients but will in the end feel impoverished and perhaps people-weary.

I know two contrasting examples of this. In one instance the worker became secretive and autonomous, sought no help from colleagues, was not supervised even while doing front-line work with abused parents and children. The eventual outcome was a court case where he himself was found guilty of abuse and sent to prison. In the other, a colleague of his, similarly without support from above but with a strong belief in her own worth and a natural ability to help clients in a personal but professional way, had enough recognition from team members and enough self-confidence to continue giving help to those who came to her.

In the end, the professional is very much alone with his or her calling and inner drive. What social workers want from their management is help to do the work. They want managers to know what they are about and what resources they need to do it well.

Once professionals are ordained or qualified, their potential for doing good or harm is great, because they are dealing with very sensitive areas in people's lives. The professional may be valued by the people he or she ministers to. But I know that, as a priest, I felt undervalued by my superiors who appeared not to be concerned about me but about matters of organization. I used to wonder sometimes how it could be that I preached thousands of sermons and that not one had ever been heard critically by my bishop or even fellow clergy. The same sort of thing tends to happen in social work. In a way this is good, because a professional should be left to get on with the job. But the risks are great too, and there is often little check on what he or she is doing. Praise or encouragement are rare but condemnation is swift if a client complains. Such accountability is indeed a safeguard against excessive freedom, and is in marked contrast to the style of the private psychotherapist who may belong to a professional association but is not obliged to undergo supervision. In an article in *The Times* of 20 February 1993, Fay Weldon writes:

> In therapy we have what amounts to a new religion, and its priests are powerful. Know Thyself Shall Be All of the Law, is their watchword. Follow us and you'll be healed, or at least saved from the hell of personal distress . . . These mind healers attempt to negate the grief and despair that is part of being alive . . . Therapists tell us not to feel guilty when we should, make us feel guilty when we otherwise would not. Consider the lot of the young working mother. It's not enough just to give birth; the child's tender psyche, according to the thera-pist, is in the mother's charge. Mother must dance attendance all the time – yet mother has to work. She needs the money. What is mother to do? Answer: she feels guilty whatever she does. Mother always feels guilty; therapists make it worse.
>
> It is the gods of therapy, suggesting to us that self-realization is our aim, that the individual need take on board only his or her problems, and let the rest go hang, who have brought about the feeling-tone (a word from therapy, and a useful one: 'What, my dear, was the feeling-tone of your dreams?') of our contemporary society. There is no such thing as society: only individuals. Morality, integrity – words that no longer apply to human conduct, but were perhaps the safest path to peace, both of the inner and the outer kind.
>
> Of course, there are therapists of great integrity and won-derful intelligence, people who spend long hours picking up and putting back together the psyches of distressed and wretched individuals. Therapists, like the rest of us, are prone to error as they burrow away in other peoples' heads . . . and without, in this country, a single law to control them; only a mass of therapeutic institutes and associations reflecting one dogma or another, self-appointed and self-policing, awarding their own certificates . . .

Both priest and social worker at least represent and carry the authority of the large official bodies to which they belong, are trained by them and obliged to carry out their policies. This offsets tendencies to idiosyncrasy on the part of the practitioner because the faithful and the public have an idea of what those policies are and so can tell when they are not being followed. What I find trying is not at all that I belong to a corps of local government officers in a social work department, but that field workers like myself belong to a system that gives orders from above rather than support from below.

There are two well known models of hierarchical order. One is the pyramid, with directives showering down, through many layers of management, on to the workers at the bottom who have to deliver the service and implement the policy, but who are not really consulted as to how this might be facilitated or improved. When cuts are made, for example, it is the service deliverers who suffer, and the clients: home care hours are lessened, eligibility for help is narrowed, Homes are closed, familiar ways of working are radically changed, teams are split up. The tiers of bureaucrats above seem not to decrease in number, managers and administrators only increase, leaving workers with more paperwork, more regulations, more frustration. There is a quotation on the wall of many social work offices:

> We trained hard, but it seemed that every time we were beginning to form into teams we would be re-organised. I was to learn later in life that we tend to meet any new situation by reorganization, and a wonderful method it can be for creating the illusion of progress while producing confusion, inefficiency and demoralization. (Caius Petronius AD 66; he was ordered to commit suicide by Nero for being a trouble maker)

This reorganization of teams has happened twice to me in fifteen years of social-work practice, and has just happened a third time with the new Community Care Act. I have been fortunate in staying in the same location with the same manager and many of the same colleagues. To others the changes are devastating. In the latest round large numbers of staff, middle managers, have taken early retirement rather than face yet another change. All their experience and accumulated wisdom has gone wasted. An Act of Parliament has simply altered the ethos of social work in one stroke.

We used to work as advocates, providers of services and resources, supporting, counselling, liaising with other authorities. Now we are Care Managers, with access to large budgets to purchase care for our clients, but with less scope for providing directly the service we were happily giving a few months ago. In my own local authority these changes have been handled as sympathetically as in any. However, the change in practice and in ethos is very unsettling. One example is to do with paperwork which has multiplied to such an extent that it takes about four times as long to fill in relevant forms as it used to.

The other model of hierarchical order is the inverted pyramid. Here, those in authority are in successive tiers below the field worker. Each tier, starting from the most authoritative at the bottom, supports the tier above so that the field worker feels able to offer enormous strength to those he tries to help. It would be wonderful if such a model could be used within the Church. The pope would then be truly what he says he is, the servant of the servants of God, rather than the head of a vast machinery of government and living in one of the grandest palaces in the world.

Similarly in local government social work, the workers at the top would, so to speak, call down to the supporters below for help with this, money for that, more deployment here, less there and so on. In any system, it seems rare to find that the people delivering the service are actually listened to so that the planners and executives can accurately provide what is really needed. They are the only ones who know, at a daily working level, what the needs are. They are the ones who face the clients.

There is an anonymous story circulating the offices, the way these amusing pieces do, and it speaks volumes:

> Once upon a time, social services and the Japanese decided to have a boat race on the Thames.
>
> Both teams practised long and hard to reach their peak performance. On the big day, they were as ready as they could be. The Japanese won by a mile.
>
> Afterwards the SSD team became very discouraged by the loss and morale sagged. Senior management decided the reason for the crushing defeat had to be found, and a project team was set up to investigate the problem and recommend appropriate action.

Their conclusion: the Japanese team had eight rowing and one person steering. Social services had one person rowing and eight steering.

Senior management immediately hired a consultancy company to do a study on the team structure. Millions of pounds and several months later, the consultancy company concluded that too many people were steering and not enough were rowing.

To prevent losing to the Japanese again next year, the team structure was changed to four steering managers, three senior steering managers and one executive steering manager. A new Quality Performance system was set up for the person rowing the boat, to give him more incentive to work harder and become a key performer.

The next year the Japanese won by two miles.

The SSD laid off the rower for poor performance, sold off all the paddles, cancelled all the capital equipment, halted the development of a new canoe, awarded high performance awards to the consultants and distributed the money saved to senior management.

A close similarity is to be found also in the two professional ways of working, proper to priests and social workers, which is that of counselling. A priest's habitat is the Church, which is supposed to have a preferential option for the poor. A social worker's is the more amorphous world of people who need help: the suffering, the deprived, the losers and the lost. I use the word counselling in the wide sense that ranges from suggested ways of seeing a person's dilemma in a different light so that it can be more easily resolved, to deeper non-directive therapeutic work that will free a sufferer to think and act positively to change his or her life for the better. The priest is concerned to help the person to become holy. The social worker is concerned to help him or her to be whole. I would not care to press either the similarity or the difference between the two words. As a matter of experience I find them somewhat similar in practice. There was a spate of letters in *The Times* last year, 'When Collars Clash', and a clergyman wrote:

> I am both a priest and a psychotherapist. Much of my work is spent trying to marry up varying relationships which some-where have gone wrong, and I also work much in the area of

loss and bereavement of one kind or another. But I do not any longer solemnize marriages or officiate at the burial of the dead: I do not work as a priest, although I happen to be one. I believe that the distinction is more important than it may seem: I sometimes explain to my patients that the authority for what we are engaged in does not lie with me (I cannot, for instance, forgive them) – they cannot, apparently forgive themselves. The authority for what we do lies somewhere in between us.

So far, I agree with him, and I am aware that vocalizing an inner conflict so that it lies in the middle there between the therapist and the client is already the healing in process. But I do not agree with his deduction:

> When, however, I come to church to hear the priest pro-nounce God's forgiveness in absolution, to meet my con-fession, I need it to come from quite elsewhere than a purely human source. Otherwise, like old John Donne, I can only complain: 'When thou hast done, thou hast not done; for I have more!' My burden is king-size, and takes the king's ransom – not the attention of the best qualified social worker or counsellor in the kingdom – to remove.

I disagree for two reasons: first, the 'king's ransom' kind of theology is not the only way of looking at the doctrine of the atonement, and I don't anyway think my burden, however guilty I am, is king-size. Only kings bear king-size burdens. And second, I know that my experience of God's love, which of course includes his acceptance and forgiveness, has come to me so often through the human love of a friend, and has brought healing in a way that nothing else did. During the bleak years as a curate when I broke down, and the equally distressing years following marriage break-down, I continued all spiritual duties more or less as usual, but I did not feel healed. In the first ordeal I was restored by the gentle, fatherly love of the aged parish priest to whom I was transferred. In the second, I came alive again because of the love of a disinterested woman who also happened to have extraordinarily well developed therapeutic skills. It wasn't her skill that healed, however, it was her love. I am not decrying confession and absolution, but I find it more helpful to regard it as a celebration of the ever available forgiveness of God when I am properly disposed to receive it, rather than as the paying of a ransom by Christ.

The beloved friend who healed me has the qualities essential for a good counsellor: honesty about the relationship, unconditional positive regard (a modern phrase, which means acceptance of the other person as he is), and congruence (which means that the counsellor's expression of words and feelings is genuine). In training students for social work I invariably come back to these qualities. If the student has them, then however limited his or her academic powers may be and however rich or narrow the experience of life, he or she will have what is essential for working with people. If not, no amount of skills and qualifications will be of much use. I know that I quite often surprise and even shock clients and colleagues because if it seems appropriate I will say and show what I feel, whether it is a home truth or a hug. It has taken me so long to be myself that I cannot easily wrap up and disguise strongly felt convictions except where I really have to. This means that trivial conversation becomes impossible, and like other people in my sort of work, I have little time for socializing and party talk. I'm happy to spend hours with someone who wants to talk in depth about their inner world, and am fortunate to have friends who dive straight below the surface when we meet. If we see much of human reality, the awfulness of some people's pain and the joy of those who have come through it, it is difficult to talk trivia about the weather and the cost of living. Perhaps that is why I enjoy Jane Austen so much: her ladies and gentlemen were stylish and self-conscious to a fault, but they were not afraid to speak out the truth to one another in words carefully couched and deadly accurate.

It is one thing to be a priest and quite another to be a cleric ordained into the Roman Catholic clerical system. Similarly, it is one thing to be a social worker with a preference for counselling, and another to be a local government officer. What I have found bemusing in both systems is that the worker is trusted too much and not enough. He is trusted to get on with the job with very little systematic oversight on the one hand, while on the other he is deluged by detailed legislation and the dreary panoply of doctrines, definitions, canon law, civil law, regulations, admonitions, protocol, procedures and the rest. They do not help much when it comes to handling a moral crisis, my own or someone else's. They do not teach me how to preach well, teach children, inspire a congregation, handle money, build a church, edit newsletters, counsel, direct, advise, cook, deal with tramps, mend gutters, raise funds and be open all hours to all kinds of people. In social work the really difficult part is to deal skilfully and helpfully with people's feelings and often unspoken needs. This work is hardly supervised, as I have said. But accountability in matters that can be measured is demanding to the point of absurdity. Everything must be done by the book and entered in triplicate. Everyone's work must be accompanied by the relevant forms which can be monitored and processed because, it seems, nobody can really be trusted. Of course any system must have some such procedures, but I think that if social workers, not to mention teachers, health workers, the police and all other public servants were trusted to be truly professional the amount of paper work and administrative staff saved could pay for more staff in the field.

Centralization tends to demoralize the professional. In the Church, various priests and theologians have identified what can further its work in Africa and South America. They have lived among the wandering tribes, the base communities, the totalitarian regimes, the oppressed and despoiled poor. They have been there for years. Vincent Donovan, Leonardo Boff, Fr Aristide, John Medcalf and Adrian Hastings are representatives of all those who know what they are talking about. They know that the only way forward is that of genuine inculturation, the choice by the communities of their own tried and proven ministers, female or male. Rome either does not listen, or it tells them to shut up. Even the forthcoming synod of African bishops is to be held – in the Vatican! A centralized authority, which is what the papal office has become in the last five or six centuries, cannot afford to trust local communities to arrange their own affairs, to let them be the Church in the actual milieu in which they live. In the same way, until very recently Moscow could not afford to let the satellite communist states run their own affairs – with some justification perhaps in the former Yugoslavia, but for what good reason in, say, the former Czechoslovakia? It is indeed ominous that I have slipped into a comparison between Rome as it is and Moscow as it was.

What many would love to see in the Church would be the resumption of real responsibility by the local bishop for the local church, where matters beyond his competence would be referred to the metropolitan or patriarch, and matters of universal concern to the pope in ecumenical or synodical council. Bishops so freed would give freedom to their local priests in turn. I am sure that, given the Catholic instinct for the good sense of the faithful (*sensus fidelium*) and for order and discipline, in communion with their bishop, they would come to balanced decisions in line with the old dictum: 'In essentials unity, in non-essentials diversity, in all things charity'. The bishop surely is the key to such a change of emphasis because he would be in close consultation both with the local church and with the wider Church. That would surely prevent the kind of enthusiastic chaos into which some charismatic and other movements have disintegrated in the past.

In an analogous way, I can't help feeling that large social services departments would do well to decentralize into very small teams with one or two workers responsible for their own patch. This model worked well in South Norfolk for many years, and the social workers became known and trusted and accessible to local professionals and clients. Norfolk Health Authority has temporarily abandoned a similar policy which devolved hospital personnel into local health centres, again with conspicuous success. We are fortunate to have such resources locally where I work, and it makes treatment easier for patients. It also gives staff a sense of belonging to the community. It is much easier for doctors and teachers, for example, if they can refer to a known worker rather than to a large office which tends to the anonymous and bureaucratic, with inevitable delay and sometimes lack of feedback about the clients.

Some years ago our social work area staff spent a two-hour meeting doing an exercise. Managers, administrative staff and field workers went off into their respective groups and were to come back an hour later with a large map of a county on which they would have drawn their model of social work as they perceived it and as they would like it to be. The results were amusing. Management drew a county with fortified keeps at all strategic points to defend them from what they called bombardment from the public. The administrators drew not a county but a grid with interlocking communication systems, but no people on it. The field workers drew an island with little towns settled among the countryside, each with its tiny office in the main street with people going in and out, and a ferry service to take paperwork to the mainland once a year.

In the end, it seems the administrators win, which is why, in the health centre where I am, all the health staff have to spend precious patient-time feeding into computers, costing many thousands of pounds, information about their work which is of no help to them and, as far as anybody can tell me, of no use to anybody else. But they are not allowed to have answering machines in their homes if they are community nurses on call. They are not given car telephones to protect them on night calls. They have no petty cash to hand out to people in immediate need. There is no money for anything practical like that.

Am I complaining just because I wanted to be a priest and not a celibate cleric, and want to be a social worker and not a care manager? Do my theologian friends complain because they want to be theologians and not cyphers for the Congregation for the Doctrine of the Faith? Do teachers complain not because they dislike teaching but because administration prevents them from doing precisely that?

If I could have one professional wish granted, it would be that everyone in a position of executive authority within the Church or Local Authority, from the very top level down (or up) should be obliged as a condition of their appointment to be responsible for a small community or a number of their own clients. It would bring realism into their decrees, and it would surely inspire and encourage their colleagues in the field and in the parishes who seldom have any animosity towards them as people, but who feel that their position in the remoteness of the Vatican, or Bishop's House or County Hall isolates them from the real needs of the people they are there to serve.

7

❧

THE PILGRIM CHURCH

When I was about seventeen and home for the holidays from the seminary, my mother was telling me about a conversation she had had recently with a lady in the village called Daisy. 'The christening in the village church was so lovely,' said Daisy, 'and your friend who is a Catholic was there as a godparent, I thought that was truly Christian of her.' 'Maybe she was a true Christian,' replied my mother, 'but she was a rotten Catholic.' Forthright as ever, she could not withhold her disapprobation of this act of disloyalty. In those days Catholics were not allowed even to pray in public with other Christians, let alone take an active part in their services. I was struck by the remark, because I thought even then that there should be no distinction, let alone contradiction between being a Christian and being a Catholic. My inner self applauded the godparent who was breaking the silly rules, but my dutiful student-for-the-priesthood self knew that my mother had the law on her side.

At about the same time my parish priest was driving me in his Austin Seven to visit the house near Abingdon where Edmund Campion had been discovered and arrested. We passed through a village and he remarked darkly: 'Over on the green lives someone who is an ex-priest.' He sounded as if he thought it was the most awful thing a man could be. I hoped the poor fellow was happy but didn't dare comment. I couldn't see why the matter was so momentous. Perhaps it was because we were going to pay our respects to an Elizabethan priest who had died in his effort to keep the old religion alive in those times.

My father was brought up in the Church of England and my mother as a Catholic. Although the former joined my mother's faith upon marriage and has remained loyal to this day, I wonder whether his outlook and that of people in the village didn't give me a sort of ecumenical outlook long before it became *de rigueur*, and an English resistance to many of the edicts of the Roman Catholic Church, spelt with a big 'R' but received by me with a small one. It is a tension I have lived with as long as I have thought independently about things. I find the ethos of Anglican worship alien to my spirit. I feel distressed whenever I walk into the magnificent Suffolk churches and see the havoc wrought by the Puritan iconoclasts; one particularly vile character called Dowsing lived near here, in Laxfield, and the beheaded statues and blank windows, whitewashed walls and empty niches bear his awful imprint to this day. Who had any right to destroy the lovely decoration that centuries of devout people had lavished upon these houses of God? So, part of me abhors what crusading Protestantism has done to what used to be Catholic England, just as what the Catholic conquistadors did to the indigenous people of South America appals me. But a big part of me loves the gentle, perceptive, tolerant kindness of many contemporary Anglican clergy, friends and relatives from whom I have learnt much and on whose goodness I have relied often.

The deeper tension for me is within my own Church. There is so much that I admire and love in it, and which has given me a rich cultural and religious inheritance, but also much that I am frightened by and ashamed of. I live with the uneasy feeling of being at ease with the *koinonia*, the communion with fellow Catholics which is sustaining and sane, and at the same time of grieving with others over the harsh, narrow, doctrinaire regime we labour under at present, which imposes unwanted, unsuitable bishops without consultation, deposes good theologians, refuses to listen to the good insights of the modern world, is patronizing towards women, cruel towards some priests who resign, takes a flat-earth attitude towards birth control, gives scant encouragement to liberation theologians and those working with the poor in South America, is ambivalent about nuclear arms, suspicious of ecumenical progress – and much else. Week after week I read of theologians who have been dismissed or forced to resign because they are thinking out a fresh approach, usually to sexual morality, and a number of friends who were priests in very good standing and who resigned honourably have been refused canonical permission to qualify as laymen. If they marry, they are officially excommunicated. Above all, I grieve the passivity of bishops throughout the world who tolerate the excessive centralization of power and control in Rome. If just one hierarchy, say, the English who are not in Rome's bad books, decided that they really do lead and represent the local church, that they foresee a serious shortage of priests in the near future and therefore simply decided to ordain married men (or even allow 'ex-priests' to lend a hand) is it likely that Rome would have the nerve to withstand them? Why do they do nothing? Why is a third of Catholic Christendom denied access to the eucharist because the pope insists on celibacy and will not allow local leaders, married or otherwise, men or women, to celebrate for the community? Why do we bishops, priests, nuns and lay people – the People of God to whom Christ bequeathed the eucharist – put up with such a nonsense? Why do I do nothing about it myself?

I suppose I do nothing because, like countless others, I have been taught at least implicitly that conformity comes before Christianity. Obedience was made to seem more important than charity or even justice. I would find it too hard to live in open rebellion with the Church I love. It is cowardly and lamentable, perhaps, but it is so. Bishops and priests who individually stand up and defy the official line are either disciplined or moved to 'safer' ground where they will not 'give scandal to the faithful'. Lay people do not stand much chance of being heard. So they tend to mine the fortress from within.

An amusing little instance of this occurred the other day. I was at the celebration of an old nun's golden anniversary. She herself rises above narrow ecclesiastical boundaries and so the church was crammed with friends both Catholic and Anglican. There was no room for anybody to move, so when it came to communion the two priests – one Anglican, the other Catholic and both wearing identical vestments, came out on to the lawn outside with separate communion cups and the people queued up accordingly. Afterwards I asked another pretty liberal nun why she hadn't helped the cause by receiving from the Anglican priest. She said with a smile that she couldn't very well, in front of the other sisters and the provincial, but she had done her bit. The woman in front of her before the queues divided was a Catholic, and she saw her heading for the wrong priest and *didn't stop her*!

Recently I re-read part of *A History of the Church* by Philip Hughes (published by Sheed and Ward). It was a standard and excellent set book when I was a student. He was describing the world into which Christianity was born and took root. Writing of Roman Imperial unity, he said that the emperor was really the chief magistrate of a city state, but 'as head of a league of similar local states, as the chief state of an Italian federation, Rome had acquired, in little more than a century and a half, in a variety of ways, province by province, the greatest of antique Empires'. The culture of the various provinces was that of ancient Egypt, or of Syria or, in Gaul, of a native Celtic civilization. Rome accepted these cultures, having a unique capacity for combining diversity in union, and the political flexibility that enabled it always to find new relationships on which to build alliances. At the same time, Rome reproduced within these regions its own model of government: that of the city.

The city was self-governing and independent of central government's bureaucracy except in the matter of gathering taxes and recruits for the vast imperial army. The empire was a federation of independent cities with their own elected magistrates. Each year there was a provincial assembly when the representative of each city came to the metropolis (not to Rome) to refer issues that could not be settled locally, and to make their complaints through the capital authorities to the Emperor. Eventually, however, a personal oath of allegiance to the Emperor was required of all subjects in authority. He directly controlled the army, and his personality became of great importance. He became in practice the direct ruler of many of the provinces, and his personal servants and bureaucrats were paid to maintain his interests and gather taxes for him. The local culture remained, but under Roman organization and rule. Eventually the local elective governments came to be of secondary importance beside the paid, Rome-appointed officials, and by the fourth century AD the Emperor had become an absolute monarch of the pre-classical oriental type.

In the field of religion there were the Roman and Greek mythological gods, anthropomorphic, reflecting the best and worst of human behaviour. Doctrine mattered little. The real affair of religion was to appease the gods through correct ritual practice:

> The Roman, in whom the notion of contract was instinctive, dealt with his gods accordingly. The appointed ritual produced the ordained effect, and all his service of the gods

> was wholly legalist, wholly formalist, the careful execution of
> man's share of the bilateral agreement. Mysticism, love of the
> gods, devotion – in the usual sense of the word – could have
> no place in such a religion, and Cicero was never truer to
> tradition that when he defined sanctity as the science of ritual.
> (Hughes, loc. cit.)

In Hellenistic paganism there was no element of grandeur, holiness, adoration or love. The focus of cult finally became the state itself, the Emperor was the object of worship and the dead Emperor was divinized.

I felt uncomfortable reading those pages because they reminded me of the imperial mentality and style of the popes and curia who in so many ways perpetuate it to this day. Vatican II clearly called for a change of direction and emphasis: the Church is to be governed by the pope-in-council, by the Bishop of Rome together with the college of bishops throughout the world. Even Vatican I had taught that, in a strictly limited sense, the pope is infallible in what he solemnly proclaims as the received teaching of the Church, but that this infallibility is no more than that which the Spirit has given to the Church as a whole. Vatican II also gave prominence to the local churches and taught that each local church together with its bishop *is* the Church, although of course, it is not the whole Church. In the same way, it taught that the fulness of Christian revelation *subsists* within the Roman Catholic Church – taking care not to *identify* Christianity with Roman Catholicism, as if to exclude the many areas of traditional Christianity to be found in other Christian traditions.

All of this was fine, but now, a quarter of a century later, it still looks and feels in practice as if the previous monarchical model of government inherited from imperial Rome and seeking to impose universal uniformity, absolute papal supremacy, conformity with Rome – all this is more important than the Vatican II model of the importance of the local churches supported by and symbolically united by the primacy of the Roman See. In theory, Rome respects local differences, local culture and traditions, the relative autonomy of the local churches under their bishops and in union with Rome. But in practice it doesn't work out like this. Every local decision has to be 'referred to Rome'. Even a hundred and fifty years ago, for instance, the majority of bishops throughout the universal Church were elected and appointed by the local church. I think I am right in saying that at the present time Rome appoints them all, and often in strong opposition to locally expressed preference and suitability. In the same way, as with the later style of the Emperors, the papal representative in each country in practice appears to carry more weight and to have more authority than the bishops' conference does.

This centralized organization undoubtedly has its strengths, and many would envy the discipline, cohesion and certainty that are synonymous with Roman Catholicism. The Church in England has, since the Reformation, had a particularly strong devotion to the Holy See. Many local churches elsewhere, in Africa for instance, have drawn strength and support from belonging to a supra-national Church with a highly visible and respected organ of government. It is surely part of the genius of the system that it acts as a counter-tendency towards narrow, selfish, isolationist local interests. Vatican II, in addition to giving due weight to the importance of the local churches, also made it very clear that each conference of local bishops has responsibilities for the universal Church as a whole. This, however, doesn't in practice seem to prevent Catholics fighting for their country and killing fellow Catholics the other side of the border.

More depressing is the uncomfortable similarity between the formalistic, ritual worship of the Roman Empire and its degeneration into Emperor worship, with the tendency in Catholicism towards a similar emphasis on ritual, on the *ex opere operato* principle of the appointed ritual producing the ordained effect, and towards a kind of worship of the pope. He is still accorded titles such as 'Most Holy Father' which properly belong to God, and there is a recent phenomenon of popes canonizing their predecessors (this pope said only last week that he hopes it won't be long before Pius XII and Paul VI are added to the ranks of saints). It is still all too familiar for us to go abroad and, at mass, hoping to find a spirit of devotion, recollection and holiness, to find instead a ritual 'gone through' with nothing to touch the human spirit and lift it for a moment to prayerful union with God or expressed love for one's neighbour.

I am trying to present the backdrop against which I have experienced the Church in my own life. I see it as a reality to be loved and deplored, proud of and critical of, grateful to and angry with.

The subject has been trenchantly dealt with by writers such as Hans Küng and Leonardo Boff in a way that does justice to the vast amount of matter. The tensions may perhaps be summarized as arising from my belonging to a Church which is both institution and movement, legalistic and charismatic, powerful and weak, all too human and not human enough, of the flesh and of the spirit. I found I couldn't, in the end, continue to hold prominent office in it, though I am happy to remain in communion with it as a layman.

The Church I am at home with is represented by people who are closely integrated into pastoral work. I find they are usually very human and immediate, at the service of others. They give and receive warmth and dignity – not the dignity of honours, titles or pre-eminence but that which arises from sincerity, truth and love. Such people tend to become liberal in outlook and in practice, perhaps not breaking the law in people's favour, but certainly bending it to breaking point. They tend to be compassionate and gentle, unjudgemental, aware of human failure including their own. They do not emphasize their authority: it is self-evident. Some have what seems to me a lamentably underdeveloped theology but they manage to put its really important themes into practice. Some of these people are bishops and priests, some are pastoral workers. The majority, of course, are lay people. Some very rarely go to church; they are living a eucharistic life in its reality already.

The Church I deplore is represented by those who are isolated from people in their community setting. They may, if they are priests, baptize and say mass, but they don't mingle outside the church door and their own front door is heavily defended. They do not visit families in their homes or children in their schools. If they are bishops they do not drop in on the priests where they work and get near to their real problems, anxieties or agonies of conscience. They are more usually to be found sitting on committees. They are always at one remove, and communicate by official letters, exhortations, legislation. They live in an ecclesiastical world that is to do with institutional proprieties: dogma, order, finance, buildings. It is not the world of the real Church, the scattered people of God trying to live out the life of the spirit in the world of the flesh.

These two kinds of Church often clash. Pastoral priests, for instance, found that services of reconciliation, ending with general absolution, were more helpful nowadays than individual confession, and were in fact bringing back thousands who had stayed away from the sacrament. Rome soon put a stop to this healthy development, in the name of a relatively recent practice – that of individual, private confession – that had fallen into disuse. Another example is that of intercommunion. In the decade after Vatican II it became increasingly common on special occasions such as weddings, retreats, conferences and ecumenical gatherings for those present to share sacramental communion together. Much good will was fostered thereby, past hurts were healed, ideological division broken down. So the practice was rigidly forbidden by Rome: people already in enough pain were told they should endure the additional pain of sacramental separation at all times.

The frightening thing about the institutional Church as such is that it becomes an end in itself, not a means to an end. Preserving it at all costs becomes the priority. Pacify dictators, negotiate concordats, remove or silence outspoken archbishops and clergy, turn a blind eye to child abuse, sexual deviancy or plain sexual activity by some of the clergy: I could give instances of all of these, just as any well informed Catholic could. This last area, of child abuse, and abuse of women, has recently become a matter of terrible concern. Numerous cases are coming to light and to the courts, in America, Canada and now in this country. The lid is off, and people are immensely hurt, ashamed, grieved and anguished as well as angry and horrified. Letters in *The Tablet* have asked again and again why the authorities have failed to act on information given to them, why they have simply sent priests elsewhere where they continue their practices? In 'Viewpoint' (*The Tablet*, 5 June 1993) Fr Thomas Faucher writes:

> What bothers me most is that there is no discernible moral outrage, no righteous indignation from priests . . . Both in my reading and in my own personal experience about how priests react, I find disturbing themes underlying the reactions, especially towards the victim who has come forward to allege sexual abuse. 'He did so only for money.' 'X is such a good priest, he shouldn't have to go through this.' 'We should pray that this embarrassment soon passes.' 'Everybody makes mistakes.' 'That was a long time ago, it shouldn't be brought up now.' 'That's what poor X gets for trying to help somebody. He makes a little mistake and gets crucified.' All these are actual quotations from priests.

Fr Faucher then goes on to look at some possible overlapping explanations for this extraordinary reluctance on the part of priests either to condemn the behaviour (not the person) or to show any interest in the victims.

> We priests are trained to forgive, to give people another chance . . . The clerical brotherhood protects its own. Usually this is called protecting 'the Church'. Any criticism of another priest would be unseemly and disloyal to the individual, the brotherhood and the institution. But this lack of reaction encourages deviant behaviour in others. One of the great unspoken clerical laws in that some topics are never openly talked about, including celibacy, homosexuality, sexual relationships or sexual abuse. In this respect the priesthood can be likened to an alcoholic or abusive family in which the members can never speak aloud what everyone knows to be true . . . To serve as a priest is a privilege, not a right. If an individual priest cannot uphold the commitments he has made, he should resign or be removed from the ministry.

I think from my own not irreproachable experience that the writer has put his finger on a significant part of the problem: that priests do not, cannot talk aloud about their sexual problems. Had we been able to do so I might possibly have been in the ministry still, and so would far better priests than I. For other reasons, I am very glad that I am not. Certainly I knew priests in high standing who were sexually active for year after year with a very large number of partners. It was an open secret, but it was never openly talked about and nothing was done.

It may just be that the coming to light of these recent abuse cases, with perhaps more to follow, as well as the universal shortage of priests, will force the issue. The Church as a whole will have to come to terms with the whole area of priesthood and sexuality, face the problems, talk about them, change the ethos of unhealthy double standards and secrecy, admit that something is very wrong with a Church that very publicly takes the high moral ground on sexual mores (why not on other mores?) while not admitting to widespread failure on the part of its ministers from the highest to the lowest to live up to the ideal themselves. To remain a priest, at whatever cost to your integrity and the ultimate good of the Church, is not a worthy cause for the Church that seeks to impose impossible burdens on lay people, homosexual men and women, the poor, the uneducated, in such matters as contraception, divorce, remarriage and so on.

Another ex-priest recently asked me how it could be possible for his former fellow priests to preach family values and practise child abuse. How could they possibly justify it to themselves? He lives in a part of Canada where his own parish priest for years abused altar boys while presenting as a warm, outgoing and likeable pastor. I do not know the answer. I indicated in earlier chapters that I myself began to lead a split life, psychologically and spiritually, and was thoroughly relieved when I resigned. I know that the capacity for self-delusion is great in myself and so, presumably, in others. When the behaviour is a mingling of sadism and ritual and piety and gross homosexuality and corruption of young children I can only say I don't begin to understand. What I do understand is that it is high time to bring skeletons out of the cupboard and look at them, to see why they got there and how they can be avoided in the future. One of the principles that seems to me to uphold a clerical system that is producing infidelity on such a wide scale, and that needs thoroughly de-emphasizing, is the *ex opere operato* principle alluded to above, with its pagan, Roman overtones of ritual correctness producing a viable covenant with God irrespective of the worthiness of the celebrant engaged in it. In theory, but not in practice, this principle has already been addressed: the theology of Vatican II has re-established the primary truth that the whole Church is a symbol of the body of Christ, and the eucharistic elements are in a way secondary symbols of that body. The theology has changed but the ethos, the structures, have not. I do not think I can improve on what another priest friend wrote to me the other week. He ought to know: he works in Peru among the poor, and it has changed his theological perspective greatly:

> The institutional Church is losing, has lost credibility. Very few people these days take much notice of a Church which insists on keeping its head in the sand, desperately clinging on to centralized authority, harassing theologians, churning out ever longer and pointless documents which no one reads and which make no difference, a Church which still largely operates on fear and secrecy and thereby promotes

dishonesty . . . fearful of change and contemptuous of the laity and frightened of women, arrogant at times in the extreme.

To say that the love of Christ, or loving Christ, is a better love than marriage is nonsense. If loving Christ is truly loving him then that must be done in the body and there cannot be any way that is better than another; it makes no sense. All the different facets of Christ's life and ministry, active and contemplative, should be expressed in the whole Church, and all activity and manner of expressing the nature of Christ in the Church is of equal value and importance, whether it is the nun levitating in her cell or the mother of seven washing her children, or dad doing the same, or the screaming distraught mother hugging the body bag of her son (Bosnia, what more powerful *Pietà* could there be than that dreadful scene?)

Because this friend has given up so much to be in Peru for the last ten years, because he has lived with the poor, learned their language in every sense, suffered and rejoiced with them, I obviously listen with care. I was with him at a talk, and someone in the audience asked him whether the poor in Peru believe in Christ(!). 'NO, they LIVE him', he shouted in reply.

I have criticized the institutional Church in its present form for various reasons, but am aware that I owe much to it also, not only my education but the gift of faith and the sense of belonging to this world and the next. I could also point out how much good is being done continually by the Church as institution, which never appears in the press.

For instance, the present bishop of my old diocese of Portsmouth has, with a devoted group of helpers, raised large sums of money for relief in Bosnia, has travelled there with some of the group and seen at first hand for himself. Such work, and there is a great deal of it going on all the time, has to be done from an institutional framework of some sort. It is the dangers inherent in institutionalism of any form that disturb me; they are bad enough in any hierarchical institutions, but should be rejected by the Church. 'With you it is not to be so' (Luke 22:26).

One of my brothers asked me to try and include in this chapter a few notes on what sort of Church I *would* like. I would like the

Church to be itself, with a much lighter centralized organization. Let it build on what is already so good: its self-confidence, universality (somewhat questionable since the break with the East in the eleventh century and the Protestant Reformation in the sixteenth), its humanity, holiness of life evidenced in so many individuals. I love its potential genius for adaptation, little developed in the last five hundred years, its monastic and mystical tradition, its rediscovery of Scripture as well as its respect for tradition. I love its incarnational, sacramental health, and its love of life, art and music. I love the ability of ordinary Catholics to laugh at themselves, and the ease with which they sense their continuity and communion with the saints of old now protecting us in heaven. I love the ordinariness and casualness with which Catholics mingle the sacred and the secular. But I would also wish the Church greatly to expand and vary its forms of ministry to include married men and women in different forms of priestly work; for lay people to be allowed officially to preach on Sundays at mass about their experience of religious life and the answers they have found. I wish the parish as a whole could really feel responsible for itself instead of acting as if it is the priest's job to be that. I would like much more emphasis on reverence and creative silence in the liturgy. I would above all wish that the Roman Catholic side in the ecumenical movement would be truly open-ended in its approach to reunion instead of giving the strong impression that it is really waiting for the other churches to fall into line and come back to Rome.

Love, and the life of the spirit are without boundaries, they transcend any religious groupings, so I wish the Church would show a greater readiness to learn from and exchange ideas with people from all the world religions who have so much to share with us, and we with them. I would like the devolution of authority back to where it belongs, to the local bishops, and the abolition of all papal nuncios and delegates, as well as the reduction of the Roman curia to a few necessary secretaries (not secretariats). I would like to see the Bishop of Rome being Bishop of Rome and not trying to be bishop of the whole Catholic world. Rome as a diocese could do with some fresh inspiration; it hardly produces any priests or religious vocations and is not a good example to the rest of Christendom. I wish that bishops were locally elected, and for a given number of years. Their curial organization would also be minimal and they would live in much greater simplicity than most of them now do in the West of Europe and the American continent.

The wider range of priestly ministers (celibate, married, part-time, full-time, work-based, community-based, parish-based, chaplains and so on) and their financial independence, if they were in paid employment, would bring advantages such as more reality-based liturgies, relevant proclamation of the gospel message, much more mutual dependence and support, less secrecy and concentration of power. I think it would lead to a laity that in turn would be less infantile and deskilled, less impotent, restless and indignant.

In various other churches many of these proposals are current practice and are seen to be having spectacular results in charismatic groups within and beyond traditional structures. What I would like would be the best of both worlds, somehow a combination of the cohesion, authority and values of the Catholic Church as it is at present, with some of the variety and vitality of smaller experimental movements which tend not to survive because they are insufficiently structured and governed. I do know that the present monolithic structure is not working.

When all is said and done, however, and it is far easier to criticize than to improve myself and be a better person within the present system, I would be happy with even relatively few of the changes indicated above, as long as the autonomy of the local bishops was assured, as well as the opening out of the other forms of ministry. I suspect I am too conservative at heart not to be moved by and to agree with Baron von Hügel's comment to his niece Gwendoline Greene:

> You see, my Gwen, how vulgar, lumpy, material appear great lumps of camphor in a drawer, and how ethereal seems the camphor smell all about in the drawer. How delicious, too, is the sense of bounding health, as one races along some down on a balmy spring morning; and how utterly vulgar, rather improper indeed, is the solid breakfast, are the processes of digestion that went before! Yet the camphor lumps, and the porridge and its digestion, they had their share, had they not? in the ethereal camphor scent, in the bounding along upon that sunlight down? And the person who would enjoy both camphor scent and disdain camphor lumps; a person who would revel in that liberal open air and condemn porridge

and digestion; such a person would be ungrateful, would she not? – would have an unreal, a superfine refinement?

The institutional, the Church is, in religion, especially in Christianity, the camphor lump, the porridge etc.; and the detached believers would have no camphor scent, no open air or bounding liberty, had there not been, from ancient times, those concrete, 'heavy', 'oppressive' things – lumps, porridge, Church.

8

FINDING GOD IN
THE WORLD

When I have helped someone through a crisis I have often been asked 'What keeps you going, who helps you?' My answer is a nutshell is 'Laughter and the love of friends', but to a close friend I would say that first and foremost prayer keeps me going. I don't mean it is a salve or balm, simply that it is the time when I feel most myself and able to draw strength from the depths of my being. My difficulty with this chapter, I can see it coming, is my inability to describe in any way that will make sense, except to other people who pray, what prayer is like. I noticed at Park Place that books about prayer always sold in large numbers. So, I notice now, do books about sex. Is it because both are such private areas of our lives, known only to God and the person who prays, or to the partners making love, that they wonder what others experience during both, and whether, therefore, they are 'getting it right'?

I learnt to pray by praying. I doubt if there is any other way. In childhood it was vocalized set prayers, litanies, hymns private or liturgical. It seemed as natural to me as breathing, and as necessary. God was always real, and access to him immediate. I felt good in his presence and came to realize that we are always in his presence and prayer is the expression of this, the wholehearted acceptance and consciousness of this. Prayer for me was, and is, like moving out of the shade and into the sun. I understand that the occupying forces in the Channel Islands built an underground hospital with no natural light, and sick people were never healed. We cannot exist healthily without light and sunshine. I cannot, without prayer. One of the distractions I had to come to some arrangement with as a student for the priesthood, and indeed in the long years as a priest, was the endless verbalization of the Church's formal offices and liturgy. If you have recited to yourself or in choir the entire psalter of 150 psalms every week of your priestly life, year in and year out; if you have intoned the words of the liturgy of the mass and sacraments hundreds of times a year; if you have said the rosary thousands of times with others or alone, you will be familiar with the double activity going on. On the surface are the words and actions, often extremely dulled by repetition (and including feelings of unworthiness therefore) and underneath is the *ostinato* which is really important, the constant recurrence of one theme such as 'I adore you'. Quite soon, I suppose when I was about seventeen, I gave up on words, ideas and images in private prayer, letting them float about if they came along, but I didn't find them any help as a general thing. I tried just to attend with my will directed to God and my whole being united with him. This kind of prayer, through no virtue of mine, has remained with me ever since. It reminds me of the old Punch cartoon in which two lovers sit on a park bench and the conversation goes: 'Darling.' 'Yes darling.' 'Nothing, darling. Just . . . darling, darling.'

These lovers felt close to each other and words were little help. Perhaps we use too many words all the time. Perhaps they cover up the truth that is too difficult to speak or better left unsaid. Perhaps they reveal our nervousness. In one of Raymond Chandler's incomparable thrillers he has his detective crouching behind a car at risk of death and coolly saying to the voluble man with the gun: 'You're nervous, people talk too much when they're nervous.' Silence, however, comes costly. It is hard to sit still and silent for a period of time. Michael Ramsey, late lamented Archbishop of Canterbury, was asked how long he prayed for and answered, 'A minute, but it takes me half an hour to get there.' We talk, says Gibran, when we cease to be at peace with our thoughts. Or when the fullness of the heart overflows.

What I find difficult about living in the 'world' rather than in the 'Church' is that I am in the midst of noise. I live in a pleasant part of East Anglia and work in a beautiful setting, but find it increasingly difficult to cope with the chatter of voices. I love a human voice when someone is speaking the direct truth or telling a funny story or recounting anything real. Words for their own sake simply drive me to distraction. It's nobody's fault, just the result of my being almost monastically trained and having now to be in the unrecollected world. It is one of the many adjustments to be made.

The adjustment that really matters is that of finding time to be in quiet prayer and also able to find the presence of God in the midst of activity. I find the balance goes like this: I usually start the day, whether at 3.30, 5.00 or 6.30, and sit bolt upright in bed as soon as I awake, absolutely still, as far as possible, for about half an hour. Sometimes it is very difficult as my mind is tormented by dreams or their hangovers, or by the prospect of the day to come. Sometimes it is easy. I try to be still, in the embrace of the unknown, unnameable One. My heart and soul go out to him. During the day that ensues I try, often without any apparent or felt success, to discern his presence. I know he is with and in other people, whether I like them or not. I know that, if I am doing my work as I should, I can do no other thing better: 'Who sweeps a room as for thy laws, makes that and th'action fine.'

I also know that concentration is a major element in loving God or neighbour, friend or spouse. So many novels, so wise in observation very often, describe the breakdown of marital harmony and it frequently boils down to this: that the woman, usually but not always, feels that her partner does not listen to her, nor does he reveal anything much of his inner self to her. She gets little attention, little time to be heard and understood. It is a precious gift we have, to give our total attention to one another. So I try, at work, to concentrate fully on the person, or even the blasted piece of paper in front of me. Some people find this unnerving – 'You are looking into my soul' has been the accusation. Most find it reassuring: someone is listening! I find that in the act of giving this attention to another person I am in the Presence. I don't know how it happens, but it is as if I am back there in the morning, sitting up and praying, totally attending. If it helps the person I am with to speak out what is troubling him or her, and myself to be equally honest, I feel a change in the atmosphere, it is a getting to the truth, and then I feel comfortable and sometimes quite high, as in prayer.

When I gave the talk that led to the writing of this book, I detailed a fairly typical day to try and exemplify how the prayer motif can continue in secular surroundings, if there are any surroundings that are secular – the world, after all, is charged with the grandeur of God. This is how the day went:

6.30	Prayer
7.00	Welcome rain; radio 3 lovely music; waking the children (it was a Monday) and talking with them, drove them to their mother, hard saying goodbye.
9.00	Pleasure at seeing colleagues after the weekend. Two of them talked in depth about themselves. Went to the bank and bumped into a distressed client, so stopped to talk.
10.00	Drove to Norwich; more lovely music.
11.00	Gave talk on bereavement to care assistants, rewarding and truthful.
12.30	Lunch and real talk with friends in Norwich.
2.30	Talked with colleagues and clients at one of our best Old People's Homes. Very warming, I think mutually so.
3.30	Support from and for colleagues at counsellors' meeting.
4.30	Took elderly client George home after his day care. He told me about his young days and why he never married – he said he didn't want to have children and them to be sent and slaughtered in a war as many of his friends were. He talked too of why he had dreaded going to the Home for day care: when he was young he used to drive mothers and children to the Workhouse, assuring them it was only for a time, knowing it was for ever.
5.00	Visit to a depressed old lady. We laughed at last.
6.00	Home. Stunning *adagio* from Serenade for thirteen stringed instruments by Mozart. I just sit and let it be Evening Prayer, better than anything I could say. 'I thought I heard the voice of God' said a later composer about this movement. So did I. I then read an item in *The Times* which wiped the prayerful smile off my face. 'A campaign to abolish secular music such as Mozart and Schubert from the Roman Catholic Mass is being led by Cardinal Biffi of Bologna . . . Delegates at the 26th National Congress of Sacred Music were told that Mozart's Masses were pretentious and Schubert's *Ave Maria* was unsuitable. The Congress was designed to 'purge the liturgy of worldly contamination', which would include the accompaniments of guitars.'

The same corner of the paper also quoted a warning from the Jesuit Roman periodical about Freudian psychoanalysis being dangerous for the public at large and for Christians in particular because of its 'materialist or pan-sexual vision of life'. So much for Mozart helping me to pray, and Freudian psychotherapy for helping other people and myself to discover the truth about ourselves.

During the rest of the day I listened to the News Quiz on Radio 4, which always makes me laugh, and prepared supper for myself and Fr James who was coming. We talked and drank wine for a long time. Two colleagues interrupted the flow when they rang up asking for advice and support. This was a particularly rich day and it provided plenty of occasions that brought me to the level of reality that I would call prayer. The most conspicuous were the meetings at a truthful level with colleagues and friends and clients, and also the times of music and silence. It is now some months since that early autumn day and as I write the flowers of spring are everywhere, primroses in the woods, cowslips in the ditches and on the banks, tulips in other people's gardens. To drive and walk through such beauty makes the divine more accessible, this coming out of the shade of winter into the light of summer. I feel the same sense of oneness with self, the universe and God when I am with my beloved friend. She makes me feel whole and at peace. For a time, time itself stands still. It is a shock to recall that when I was seventeen I was not allowed to read what the poets and novelists say about human love. Like the other students, I was supposed to care only for the love of God, as if he were not incarnate nor always revealing himself in the continuing creation of all things. The *Imitation of Christ* was required reading, on the other hand, and although it is full of good things there is also a strong suspicion of worldly love as if it were the enemy of the divine: 'As often as I have been among men I have returned less a man.' I usually find exactly the opposite.

In the day outlined above there was little pain, apart from the abiding pain I and so many people suffer of being separated from the loved ones I want to be with and being with the people, sometimes, that I would rather not be with. But in times of suffering, and they are many, I am also conscious of somehow living at a deeper level of understanding and union with the incarnate suffering and glorified God. It is richer than feeling nothing, better than bored indifference. It forces me to be passive, to do nothing except wait until I can be with them again. It reminds me of a complete dependence on God that success obscures. I feel nearer to reality and the truth about the human condition. And I know that sorrow will somehow be turned into joy, as Jesus said.

In contrast to these moments of felt union with the divine are those when I feel out of touch with God, when instead of harmony, warmth and creative pain I am in the midst of distraction, disharmony and coldness. It is like listening to 'On Air' and being switched from Gluck to Berg.

Distraction is the opposite of concentration and makes me feel alienated and irritable as if I am missing the mark. There are small examples of it when the words or music of a hymn at mass are ugly, banal, cheap and trivial. There are the daily examples of it in broadcasting, the gobbledegook of the weather forecaster's language and extraordinary voice, the patronizing sentiment of the advertisers, the mindless rubbish children watch on television (no worse, I suppose, than the comics of my own childhood). There is the invasion of noise wherever we go, it sometimes seems. Even the lovely beamed pubs in Suffolk have this awful canned Muzak all the time. I sit in the garden instead with my own beer, and am driven indoors by the barking of leashed dogs or the transistors of neighbours.

Much more important and not so easily avoided are the times when I feel out of harmony with people. What I fear is having my motives misunderstood, so that what was meant as a kindness is interpreted as an intrusion or worse. Until I have been able to explain myself and be accepted I feel wretched and separated. If it is indeed my fault I also feel wretched until I have put it right as far as possible. When there is no way of putting it right I can only ask forgiveness and hope I have learnt yet another lesson. In the same way, I am frightened of anger, in others and in myself. I have not yet learnt how to be angry in an effective or appropriate way, except on rare occasions when I feel my case is genuine and mind very much about it. I know this is an area of myself that I must somehow learn to use constructively, otherwise it will continue to be 'unredeemed', that is, part of the reality of being human and fallible but still not open to God. As long as anger in others or myself is not acknowledged and usefully channelled, that area will be a no-prayer area. But how, for instance, can I deal with the anger I feel when forced to spend time on unproductive, repetitive, wasteful paperwork when I feel I could be doing better things?

Coldness is a quality I have mentioned before quite often. I find physical coldness hard to put up with, perhaps because of what it symbolizes as much as for its own harsh reality. It makes me feel far from God, as it did one of the heroic survivors of the plane crash when the young South American rugby players were trapped in the snow for seventy-two days. When I encounter the coldness of an administrative machine, of a heavily defended person, of unsmiling people in power and authority, of rejection – at these times I feel isolated, diminished, unreal and again out of touch with God. I fear, too, those reformed Christian religions that prefer whitewash, plainness and formality to the more typically Catholic colour, decoration and ebullience in architecture and liturgy. Baroquery may well be over the top at times, vulgar, garish and obtrusive, but it seems to me alive and warm like really human beings are, not sanitized and sterile and tidy and dead.

I was thinking about these things, as one does before writing a chapter, and happened to read again an article in *The Tablet* of 6 March 1993, written by Joyce Huggett, and part of a series called 'How I Pray'. She writes in essentially the same terms of finding stability in her life by the use of four approaches. These are con-templation – becoming still and soaking in the love of God; the practice of the presence of God, which she calls 'connectedness'; compassion – contemplatives shouldn't be so heavenly minded that they are of no earthly use; community prayer – we cannot believe and love and pray indefinitely on our own; we are a people, a body, a Church.

Perhaps I may pause on that word 'Church' for a moment and ask what help it is to me in the search for union with God in the world. As for many Catholics, the week for me begins and ends with mass on Sunday and I rarely miss it. Whether the singing and the sermon are uplifting and sublime, or cacophonic and tedious (more usually the latter), whether the babies are peaceful or noisy, whether special friends are present or absent, I invariably come away with a profound sense of wholeness renewed, of a week for which I have given thanks and a week to come which has been offered and consecrated with the bread and wine. In a sense, although they can help or hinder on the surface, words and music don't matter so very much; it is the act of being there, part of the corporate, tangible, flesh-and-blood universal Church locally manifested and loyally turning up yet again to share their love of God in Christ together – that is what matters. I think it is also the vision thing, which I find difficult to describe. For an hour a week I am no longer Anthony, English, a social worker, living in Suffolk, father of three, friend of many, praying alone. I am a member of the universal *ecclesia christiana et catholica*, united with Christ and his saints past and present, believing and doing and hoping as they did and do, pooling my small contribution with their massive self-giving, buoyed up by them, one with them in a way that is about as matter-of-fact as it could be. The sort of people I meet at mass are exactly the sort of people I see in the High Street and they look it: no very special clothes, no very great apparent reverence, but the sense of concentration, the feeling of prayer, the good will, the sense of belonging are often intense and always enriching.

Another more subtle way in which I am often reminded of being a Catholic and therefore helped to try and be a better one, is that so many people I daily encounter either know I am one, or it emerges in conversation. This often brings about a discussion of religion, sometimes controversial and embarrassing ('Did you see that programme on Catholics and Sex last night?') and sometimes seriously religious ('Can you advise me how to help this friend with religious hang-ups?').

The Church helps too because it provides an ample framework and support for my life, so that I feel free to put energy into living rather than in worrying about ultimate questions, looking for meaning, wondering whether it's all worth it. I'm not saying non-religious people do that, but I think I would if it weren't for the Church. In that sense I never feel isolated. Nor do I feel the need for each day to justify itself. If I have failed, if people were out when I called, if paperwork has been mislaid, if letters are unanswered and so on, it doesn't really matter; the day doesn't depend for its success on what I achieved but only in what I tried to achieve. Of course I get irritated like everybody else by wasting time, being under-used, being without any power to change the way things are or put something right because the system won't allow for it. Of course I feel diminished by disparagement, hurt by neglect, surprised by ingratitude. I know deep down, however, that none of it really matters because the whole thing is in God's hands, I am not at all essential but at the same time I am justified – not because I have achieved or failed but because I am loved by God. This really does help to keep everything else together and in a perspective that will not indefinitely allow for discouragement, let alone for despair. I often think it is ironic that the Reformation was to some extent about the Reformers' objection to the Catholic belief in good works. No, they argued, faith is all that matters, not works. In practice it is so often Protestant attitudes that lead to a scrupulous and exhausting work ethic as if everything depended on human effort, and it is Catholic attitudes that keep work firmly in its place as a creative expression of trust in God but not a means to faith in self or God.

Committed Catholics are in no sense self-made people. They will tend towards laziness perhaps, letting God do the work they ought to be doing, but they will also tend to be somewhat relaxed, knowing that everything does not depend on them. Perhaps I am talking of extremes, and probably most people are a fair balance of faith and works. What I find refreshing about the Church, and I hope it colours my everyday life, is a certain lack of earnestness, that everything has got to be done today. Many of the most relaxed people I know are very hard-working monks and nuns and lay people in the caring professions who indeed work as if everything depended on them but temper it by praying as if everything depended on God.

As if everything depended – and yet I deeply respect Eric Fromm's work, and in *The Art of Loving* (HarperCollins, Mandala, 1985) he writes:

> The truly religious person does not pray for anything, does not expect anything from God . . . he knows nothing about God . . . God becomes to him a symbol in which man, at an earlier stage of his evolution, has expressed the totality of that which man is striving for, the realm of the spiritual world, of love, truth and justice . . . he thinks truth, lives love and justice, and considers all of his life only valuable inasmuch as it gives him the chance to arrive at an even fuller understanding of his human powers – as the only reality that matters, as the only object of ultimate concern and eventually he does not speak about God, not even mention his name. To love God, if he were going to use that word, would mean, to long for the

attainment of the full capacity to love, for the realization of that which 'God' stands for in oneself.

Is the God I seek to be one with in daily life just a symbol? And if he is more than that, am I not, according to Fromm, a truly religious person? Eckhart (for whom I have an even greater respect than for Fromm, and not merely because his writings were condemned by the pope in 1329) wrote: 'God is the absolute Nothing.' But he also wrote:

> If you love yourself, you love everybody else as you do yourself. As long as you love another person less than you love yourself, you will not really succeed in loving yourself, but if you love all alike, including yourself, you will love them as one person and that person is both God and man. (*Meister Eckhart*, trans. R B Blakeny: London, Watkins, 1955)

Behind these quotations from both writers lies a perspective that is strange to many of us. It is not easy, perhaps not possible to conceptualize, indeed it is against conceptualization. Fromm, I think convincingly, traces the origins of the conceptual basis of Roman Catholicism and of science (both of which he implies are aberrations) as logically resulting from Aristotelian logic. At its most basic, this is the proposition that A cannot be A and non-A. A very different tradition is to be found in the thought and philosophy of Eastern logic and in the language of Heraclitus and the mystical (Christian, Buddhist and so on) writings of the Middle Ages. This is what he calls paradoxical logic, and it means that opposite qualities may be predicated at the same time about the same subject. As the former tradition is more than familiar to us, let me quote what Fromm says about the latter:

> The paradoxical standpoint led to the emphasis on transforming man, rather than to the development of dogma on the one hand, and science on the other. From the Indian, Chinese and mystical standpoints, the religious task of man is not to think right, but to act right, and/or to become one with the One in the act of concentrated meditation . . . The opposite is true for the mainstream of Western thought. Since one expected to find the ultimate truth in the right thought, major emphasis was on thought, although right action was held to be important too. In religious development this led to the

formulation of dogmas, endless arguments about dogmatic formulations, and intolerance of the 'non-believer' or heretic. It furthermore led to the emphasis on 'believing in God' as the main aim of a religious attitude. This, of course, did not mean that there was not also the concept that one ought to live right. But nevertheless, the person who believed in God – even if he did not live God – felt himself to be superior to the one who lived God, but did not 'believe' in him.

In scholastic jargon, orthodoxy was more important than orthopraxis, right belief more important than right behaviour. It found its *reductio ad absurdum* in Luther's saying '*Pecca fortiter sed crede fortius*' ('Never mind if you sin a lot as long as you believe a lot more'). It is still alive and well – if that's the correct word! – as instanced by the present Principal of the Jesuits who wrote:

> In the noviceship it was drummed into us to observe and fulfil our 'spiritual duties' with meticulous scrupulosity. They were ever given pride of place on the daily agenda, taking precedence over everything else. We even used to joke that a person could be uncharitable, selfish, bigoted, rude or just insufferable but, as long as he did not miss morning oblation (prayer) he was considered a good religious. ('How I pray', *The Tablet*, 4 April 1993)

Fromm is not an atheist any more than is Eckhart, though their language may seem to indicate it because it is unfamiliar to pious modern ears. He does not believe in the transcendent spiritual realm as if it were only spiritual in so far as man has developed truth, love and justice by his own efforts.

Paradoxical logic allows me to see God simultaneously as the One and the Many, the one who cannot change and ever changes, the impassive and the suffering God, the almighty helpless one. Whatever my belief structure, and it has been shaped by and depended for growth on fifty years of Church teaching through all its ecclesiastical apparatus. I have for long been convinced however, that it matters much more what a person does than what he or she believes. But here I find myself splitting again. On the one hand I know and believe in the unknowable God, about whom it is as meaningless to say that he (she) changes as it is to say that he (she) is unchangeable, because human language cannot speak of the divine except in analogy and we really do not know how far the analogy goes, we only know God as reflected in and, as it were, filtered through our created world and perceived through our human senses. On the other hand, as part of the reflection and filtering, there is the revelation of God in Christ, the culmination, as Christians believe, of his revelation through the religious people anteceding Christ. Jesus revealed a God who is intensely personal and has definite attributes: he is trustworthy, forgiving, concerned and so on. So at times I find myself sitting and praying before the God who is absolutely nothing, silent, helpless, both of us (if I may dare to put it like that). At other times, as at mass, I quite comfortably predicate all sorts of qualities of him and pray for help in all sorts of ways, to forgive my sins, to bless my loved ones. I am also painfully aware that even if my belief is orthodox, it is fruitless unless it leads me to act justly and love tenderly. My belief won't 'save' me at all, my crying 'Lord, Lord', even if my definition of the Lord could withstand the scrutiny of the Congregation for the Doctrine of the Faith, which I'm sure it could not. I am equally aware that, as Christians murder Christians in Bosnia at present, and have done throughout the often shameful history of Christianity, right belief is no guarantee at all of right behaviour.

I find myself coming back to some kind of *modus vivendi* between these extremes of an unknown God and a God defined down to the last detail, if that were possible, by any rigid system of theology including Catholic ones. It is to concentrate as far as I can on living accurately, in the present moment, as creatively as I can and as generously as my selfish nature will allow. At any given time I cannot see that there is any other way to find him than by wholly attending to the work in hand, the person I am with, the problem to be addressed, the music to be listened to. I don't know where else to find life, reality, self, God. This brings its own discipline which is severe enough for my comfortable tastes, because it makes the present moment intensely happy and fulfilled or equally miserable and frustrating. I cannot easily temper the first by remembering what will lie beyond, nor the second by realizing that it too will pass.

I am not in any way trying to pretend that I succeed in living in the present, waiting before God, attentive and undistracted, peaceful and prayerful. Anyone who knows me would laugh at the idea. But what I do value is the discovery that took me, anyway, some time to learn, which is that I do not have to leave the world of human affairs, the stuff of daily life, this kind cruel universe of good and evil, in order to be with God. He is present all the time, and if I am attending to what seems to be his work or pleasure, then I am indeed waiting on him and somehow in union with him.

Gibran comes to the end of *The Prophet* having spoken eloquently about love and marriage, work and rest, joy and pain, parenting and friendship. A listener said: 'Speak to us of religion', and he answered 'Have I spoken of aught else?' I feel grateful that I have travelled at least far enough on the hopeful journey to fulfilment to have realized, however imperfectly, that God is to be found in ordinary daily life, and that I do not have to be extraordinary or do unusual religious antics, or adopt this or that 'way' – it is all there, ready to hand in the human business of living. But I also know that for me the prayer at the beginning of the day is the only possible way I shall have much chance of encountering God on the journey through it, because if I start in the morning being distracted I shall probably continue like that till bedtime. I would encourage anyone who thinks they are not religious enough to ask themselves first whether they are human enough. If they are, perhaps the rest will take care of itself.

EPILOGUE:
TO TRAVEL HOPEFULLY

It is difficult to know how to end. I am still travelling and have to admit that I must come to terms with not having what I think I want. In my ideal world I would be living with the woman I love and would also be doing some kind of priestly work locally. In reality I am not officially allowed to do either, my marriage having long since broken down and priesthood abandoned. It is ironic that after what I have learned from both experiences I would probably be much more qualified to live generously in a partnership, and would bring to a pastoral role all kinds of qualities and a range of sympathies I was not capable of before.

What, therefore, can I do? I can and do give and receive much in loving my beloved friend, my children and many friends and relatives. I can and hope I do receive much from the Church and use whatever opportunities are offered to give talks to various groups and to support individuals who come for counselling. I can and do pray.

I am not able to feel complacent or settled or complete. I live, most of the time, alone. I do not wish it or like it, but I can use it to develop the inner life and to provide refreshment for weary friends who come to stay.

So many people are in this position: the bereaved, in short. Nobody speaks for them much. We are on the margins and do not often get invited out socially. But we can still be fully alive and so become the glory of God. We have freedom to be available, leisure to read, time for friendship. We have what many priests and married people would envy, our liberty. It is, to be sure, not a lot of fun when we are ill, or depressed, hard up or lonely. It is not very easy

119

going on holiday with the children (men as single parents aren't recognized), going to weddings, finding the motivation to clean the house, do the garden or a thousand other things. But it is certainly possible, and every form of life has similar difficulties.

The greatest gift in my experience of failure and picking up pieces is that I now take very little for granted. A visit from a friend, a week or two with the children, times with my own brothers, sisters, aunts, time with my beloved, time with God – these are satisfying, sometimes ecstatic and always good. Does it really matter if my vocation in the end is to have no vocation except to try and live the good and hard times to the full? Don't we all have to do that anyway?

Arrival can mean inertia, boredom, calm, peace, sterility – whatever you make it. Travelling hopefully can mean enterprise, interest, restlessness, agony, fruitfulness, loneliness, joy – what you make it.

I hope that what I have written, at some cost and at the risk of sounding like a dog in the manger, may at least encourage some of my patient readers to know that there are many of us who feel we could and should do more but who are in fact called simply to be content, and to be grateful for what we have.

BIBLIOGRAPHY

Dominian, J, *Marital Breakdown* (Penguin Books).

Meister Eckhart, trans. R B Blakeny (London, Watkins, 1955).

E Fromm, *The Art of Loving* (HarperCollins, Mandala, 1985).

P Hughes, *A History of the Church* (Sheed and Ward, 1948).

K T Kelly, *Divorce and Second Marriage* (Collins, 1982).

A Matthews, *Lipstick on the Host* (Secker, 1992).

J H Newman, *An Essay on the Development of Christian Doctrine* (Longmans, 1845).

E Schillebeeckx, *Ministry: A Case for Change* (SCM, 1981).

Baron F von Hügel, *Letters to a Niece*, Gwendoline Greene (ed.) (London, J M Dent and Sons, 1928).